THE *Diary* OF A *Soul*

THE Diary OF A Soul

Alicia Bella Paneque

and

Vellucci Luigi

Copyright © 2021 by Alicia Bella Paneque and Vellucci Luigi.

Library of Congress Control Number: 2021919975

HARDBACK: 978-1-956803-18-1
PAPERBACK: 978-1-956803-17-4
EBOOK: 978-1-956803-19-8

Ordering Information:

For orders and inquiries, please contact:
1-888-404-1388
www.goldtouchpress.com
book.orders@goldtouchpress.com

Printed in the United States of America

Many events, many small details follow one another in this diary of the soul and on the whole, they build the plot of an entire existence, retraced, moment after moment, in successes, hopes, dreams, and expectations. A life made of dedication to children, to a house that so often dissolves, like hopes, like loves. And it is increasingly difficult to reconstruct that dream of reunited family, solid as the five fingers of the same hand, or who knows of a love: in which the protagonist believes, deludes herself, hopes to find so many times, even to give a father to her children for whom she will always sacrifice herself, her pride, dreams even. And those happy moments reappear in Rome when Alicia becomes Bella the actress, protagonist contested by mythical characters and, between Hercules, Manistee and Samson, life becomes fantasy, luxury, wealth, satisfaction and then this life becomes, sometimes, a tacit regret: that of having abandoned cinema, career and the way of success, economic well-being, if surrounded by men who have grasped only the appearance, beauty, not the soul and then threw it away unscrupulously, without love: that love that Bella needed to live. The different love is alternate, the moments of a life retraced sometimes bitterly, sometimes with a smile on the lips and the grit of those who face them with courage and, sometimes, in the hope of escaping reality, of building the dream again: a simple reality surrounded by people loved forgiving even those who, as a child, abused it. She continues to give up on herself, moving from one experience to another in order to give her children a home and a father figure that, even this one, will prove to be a bitter disappointing reality made of anger and crying. Una continues to struggle to live and overcome small and large obstacles: one husband degenerate and another mentally ill and then another episode that I leave to the reader. The key to reading this sincere, touching autobiography lies precisely in this desire to always fight of the protagonist, fight to survive and find herself, day after day, caressed now only by the smile of her daughter, by her nieces and who knows from her own dreams. Reading this story, told in the simplest and most sincere words, makes us know not only the protagonist of many stories of peplum cinema but, even more so, makes us love her good soul as a true woman in her struggle for existence. And I'd like to end with the same words as Alicia or if you want Bella Cortez. "For now, my story ends here but continues silent in a romantic dream that, left secret in the drawer of the heart, I would like to have told by a single pen more valid than mine, by a good writer. For now, this belongs to a dream." Luigi Felucca - Wikipedia

An Interview

There's a wind tonight; a wind that comes from the sea; the sea of memories; some lost, forgotten by memory, others resurface, as in the clouds, to make you smile again or take you so far, back in time, in moments of ancient sorrows, boundless anxieties and even joys of love when sometimes the wind subsides, the clouds disappear on the horizon and the sun returns.

And now after so many years, a famous journalist, the writer Jack La Motta, asked me to interview me, to tell him my story as a woman and an actress. So, I reopen the door of the past to review my life in Italy in cinema but also the memories of my childhood and those that, later, the years have given me so far.

When he came in, like a gentleman of old, Jack kissed my hand. We sat down, drank coffee, and then he started asking me questions for his newspaper.

Tell me about his childhood there in Cuba, his affections, his parents, and tell me about the essential moments of a lifetime.

From that telling resurfaced my life. "You remember it as if it were of another person, as if it were just a story." Jack suggested.

"I see myself as a child, over there, in Cuba, in that small country and I almost see, before the eyes that perhaps only imagine the story of my father and mother, even from episodes told to me by them when I was so small, yet I perceived, at times, the sense of destiny."

In the Eastern province of Cuba, in a small town called Niquero, lived a woman named Eleodora Fuentes. She was a Caribbean Indian who was widowed with eight children. Her husband suffered from epilepsy and one night, while sleeping in a hammock, outside the open-air house - after a tremendous binge - she had an epilepsy attack, and unfortunately fell into the fire that had prepared to warm up and practically burned alive, because no one could help him.

In another place, in the same city, lived a man named Ramón Paneque y García, who came from a family of islanders and who had remained widowed. His wife, after giving him five children, died of tuberculosis, a very contagious disease that he unintentionally passed on to his children.

Ramón was a hard-working farmer, he had his own farm, which was very productive, but he needed a woman to help him raise children.

And in a dance that the community held for the end-of-year festivities, Ramón and Eleodora met, fell in love and soon got married, thus creating a large family with that battalion of boys.

Thus, they began a new life and, over the years, four of Ramón's children, three males and a female, died from contagion of the disease inherited from their mother, leaving only one of the females and children of Eleodora. Meanwhile, Eleodora and Ramón had other children, the last of whom is Alicia, the protagonist of this story, who later changed her name to that of Bella Cortez, with whom she became known in cinema. In that country Bella worked in eleven Italian films in all the southern and northern parts of Italy, in Trieste, on the border with Yugoslavia and also in Turkey, Greece and Iran. And when Bella married her French Robert F. Poitevin, they traveled a lot, to Paris and the French Riviera, to Nice and Monte Carlos, and Saint Tropez. After having her first child, she moved to New Jersey, very close to New York, where her husband worked and while attending a school where she learned Key Punch and spoke English. Alicia's story- my story -begins with my mother's death, when she's only five years old.

Jack interrupted my talk to suggest:

"You have to see each other as a child, on your father's farm, and describe those places, those moments of your life, in the present but with your eyes of that time."

He had Jack, the ability to put me at ease and make me tell many episodes of my life, making me go back in time, as if the past returned to a vision that became present: moments lived that became alive, still alive.

Jack was not only an established journalist and writer but unwittingly perhaps a psychotherapist. He understood that in telling my story, I relived the past, I suffered it but I overcame the pains, disagreements, injustices suffered and I freed myself by acquiring a sense of peace and serenity that a single look and a smile of his made me live again and who knows to dream again …

That evening he advised me:

"Use the present as if, in trance, rivedessi, your childhood, child's games, your little dreams."

And I really see the past as if it wasn't me. I watch it almost like a movie.

On my father's farm, I see the memories of that time... From the top of a vedhill or a cultivated land of considerable size, in the middle of which is a wooden house, painted in a light brown color. At the front of the house there is a large tree, where children play on a swing that hangs from a branch. There are 50 mango trees and when I fall to the ground, I am afraid because underneath it is dark, at the bottom of the side of all banana trees, and in the highest part many pine trees (pineapple). In order not to sting me cautiously in crossing those places so rich in thorny plants. Between the pine forest stands and even larger ground, a path takes me to the end of our property, where my father caught a beaten corn and cotton plants which I use to make the hair of dolls. I see my mother feeding the chickens, turkeys and pork. Then, in front of the house grows its flowers of tropical plants. And already you hear it and the zufolare of the train, in the nearby railway... And right next to the railway is that lawn, where, in the green Domingo pasture, the beautiful all-white horse, along with the cows that look tired in their slow walking and the black bull looks at them and is not at all docile.

I see a five-year-old girl in the house feeding domestic birds raised in the yard. He has black hair and dark brown eyes, almost like those of Asians, his mouth and nose are so well formed, and harmonize the face of beauties in that small body.

When the little girl finishes feeding the animals, returned to the house and with a needle with thread begins to make a necklace of watermelon seeds and once finished jumping and running, she goes where the children play with the swing and show them the finished necklace and with an air of satisfaction office:

It's for my mom.

So, he runs into the house until he's out of sight with the other kids.

I see my picture again. That little girl is me... In the humbly arranged bedroom of the house, there is a copper bed where a woman of about forty-four years lies; she has tanned skin, her long black and smooth hair, very similar to my hair. From the eyes and face shines through the suffering of this unfortunate woman sick to death.

"Mom, get this necklace, I did it for you."

"Thank you, love, but what happens then... is it so sick to?"

"Don't worry, Mom, you're going to be fine soon."

With a sad look and deep sorrow in her voice, my mother tells me:

"Bring me the green white flower dress that's in the chair and also the belt."

I almost run to bring her the dress, together with the belt of the same fabric and in front of her I ask her:

"Are you going to get dressed to go out?"

"Yes daughter, but I appreciate you going out so I can change and now the emotion was so strong that I couldn't tell it like it wasn't my story." It was me Alicia and I was suffering by telling, and so I continued:

"Once I left the room, my mother took her belt from one end and tied her to the bars of the bedhead and the other end tied it to her neck, then, taking a deep breath, tried to drop the body down into hanging, but the weakness, caused by cancer of over a year, prevented her from carrying out that painful action, produced by despair and impotence. This attempt produced indescribable pain forcing her to sound an anguished cry."

-Ayyyyyyyy, my God!"

And now I see again, as from afar those moments...

At the cry of her mother, the girl who was out of the room, entered. She had an expression of surprise and fear on her face at the same time and as if she understood the danger her mother was going through, looked at her with the pain reflected on her face and put her hands in her mouth to silence a scream that, despite everything she then uttered. He ran desperately through the countryside screaming and crying as he called his father. He knew where to find him and when he finally found him, he could barely speak and among the sobs told him what was going on.

Dad, Mom squeezed a headband around her neck and almost fell out of bed.

The father said nothing, did not answer her and, without wasting time, ran home.

When they arrive, they see reality: the mother who tried to kill herself but failed, and now desperately tries to take his belt off his neck as he cries.

"I don't want to live on, I'm in a lot of pain, I can't stand this torture anymore. I know that the operation they had a year ago was useless and that the cancer has reproduced again."

Ramón consoled her and asked her for patience:

"Try to be patient, I promise I'll talk to the doctors who followed you during the operation to get you to use other drugs, see what to heal soon."

After a short time, one afternoon, when Alicia returned from her school, she found the house full of people, friends and neighbors commenting on her mother's death. Eleodora Fuentes de Paneque had died at the age of forty-five, ending a long suffering.

Among other comments, what was most felt among the funeral participants was always the same:

"What about that little girl who isn't even six years old?"

Alicia had a half-sister from Eleodora's first marriage. She was twenty-four years old, married and living in Havana, the capital of the island of Cuba, and when she learned of her mother's death, she came to the funeral and thinking of her younger sister, she proposed to Ramón to take King Alicia to live with her and her husband.

After collecting her few having's, Alicia greets her father with a kiss, not knowing that this would be the last act of affection between the two of them.

Already sitting on the bus with the words "Habana Manzanillo and Manzanillo Habana", she looked out the window, as if trying to record the face of her father who was dismissing her. Among his hands he still had the melon seed necklace he had given his mother and the sad expression on his face became more evident when the bus left leaving the countryside and all his memories.

But the memories, not at all happy, made me talk to myself again...

My sister often revealed her malice towards me, with mistreatment not only verbal but also with absurd physical punishments that embittered me even more because I certainly did not feel loved.

He made me clean the house, do my laundry and cook while er or even a little girl and if I didn't do it or well, he would put raw rice or dry corn on the floor where I had to be on my knees. Other times he hit me with a belt.

It was a pleasure for me to go to school, but I didn't say anything about what was happening at home. School was like an oasis of peace, wherever my playmates and studies. I stayed there until I was 17. Then I went to live in Europe, where he learned about other cultures and also learned to speak Italian and French.

The Meeting With The Agent
Of The Italian Film

That day I got by taxi to the Hotel National where I worked. I was 16years old and started working the day before, studying at night with my brother at the Vedado Institute, near where he lived.

It was a hot summer morning, stay or walking to my work with the spiky and proud safety of my body so sinuous and sensual and turning in the hotel, two foreigners (Italians) approached me. Renato Spera and Conte Vasselli, who distributed Italian films in Havana. Con the smiling but slightly surprised face greets the newcomers and chiedo:

"How can I help you?"

They, after having done the paperwork to stay, start talking to me.

"What's your name?"

"Alicia Paneque, at your service"

"We've been watching you and you won't believe it, but we're sure you have the image of a movie actress."

Renato Spera had spoken to me and Vasselli then continued:

"Would you like to be an actress in Italian cinema?"

I didn't believe it and in an explosion of joy remarried:

"Yes, but I'm a minor and I can't leave the country without my father's permission, and I don't know anything about acting."

"It's not a problem, we can fix it. Before you start working, you'll go to an academy of dramatic and film art. We can also talk to your father."

"Really? So, I have to go to my father's house to ask for his permission."

"Yes, of course."

The next day I was traveling by taxi to the El Vedado district, in the city of Havana, where my father lived. While Renato and Vasselli were speaking in Italian, and I, who did not understand them, took me away from my thoughts towards the last meeting with my father in Niquero, seven years after my mother's death, I was returning to our old woman at home.

When I got there the first thing, I saw was the big tree in front of the house, where I had or played so many times swinging on the swing and when I came to the house, I met my stepmother, Caridad and a five-year-old half-sister, who in the face looked like my father, but the hair was that of his mother of an intense red and curled without combing; they were both barefoot. I thought:

"What a big difference there is between this woman and my mother!"

In the house were two sons of Caridad, from his first marriage: Ambrosius, seventeen, and Elvira, thirteen.

It wasn't long before I realized that she wasn't loved by the new inhabitants of the house and that she wasn't welcome and, to make matters worse, one afternoon when she inadvertently returned home and found me unwittingly seeing my stepmother - unfaithful to my father- with a family friend.

On the same night as the accident, after the meal, Caridad and Ambrosio decide to get rid of me and when they go to bed, the stepmother begins her plan. Caridad told Ramón that I have relations with his son and Ambrosio, according to his mother's plans, had a mission to enter the room and lie next to me, but he woke me up and he covered my mouth so as not to scream, as he looked towards the door as if he were waiting for someone.

A few minutes later Ramón came in with a broom in his hand to hit him while insulting me. When I realized what was happening, he pushed the Ambrosio, but he fell on Ramón and took advantage of the confusion to jump out of bed and grab his clothes.

"I'm not the one who dishonored this house, but your wife, I saw her and I also listened to the conversation she and Ambrose had, planning what happened tonight."

Ambrosio restrained Ramón so that he wouldn't hit me while here plied:

"I don't believe anything you say, get out of here!"

And I look at the boy and sobbing at the dissi:

"I'm leaving, but not before you tell my dad the truth."

Ambrosio response "Yes, I will."

At dawn, when my father left, he started picking up my clothes and going to another sister's house until he raised the money for the return ticket to Havana. -

I had retraced the moments of a past that had come back to my mind and when Renato and Vasselli finished talking and turned to me, they had to call me several times to get me back to the present.

"Siam or arrived?"

Almost replied "Vasselli."

When they arrived in El Vedado, the meeting with my father was short, tense and somewhat controversial, Ramón was reluctant to give me permission because I was a minor, but the presence of my brother, who supported the idea, helped me a lot by saying a phrase that later made history.

"Communism is already on the island's doorstep; you'd better go live in a free country, you're sure to be better-off."

There's nothing more to say," Ramón said.

Thanks to that phrase of my brother, Ramón agreed to authorize me to travel out of the country.

Havana Airport

C ount Vasselli and Renato Speraleave for Italy and I accompany them to the airport. They would send me the ticket to go to Rome.

Renato gave me the permission signed by my father, with whom I had to make the documents for the passport.

"You have to behave very cautiously, don't talk to people you don't trust about this project and don't worry, we're sure it's going to be very good for you."

And after many other recommendations, they greeted me.

I wasted no time and started the procedures to obtain the documents required for the issuance of the passport. While I was in my apartment, I spoke to two young friends and told them about my plans.

"I'm already going to get my passport, now I'm waiting for my ticket to Italy, so I'll drop you off."

"We wish you the best for your trip, I hope all your dreams come true and don't forget about us."

After all, maybe they didn't believe me; they thought mine was just a dream.

Soon I received the ticket, took my bags, a taxi and away to the airport. From the windows on the second floor, my friends greeted me and watched the taxi move away until it was no longer seen.

May God always accompany you?

And now look at it or towards infinity, as if trying to get there by taxi.

Rome Airport

Renato Spera and Conte Vasselli were waiting for me impatiently.

The flight route was Havana to Miami; Miami from New York; New York to Paris and Paris to Rome, the estimated flight time was eighteen hours, but it seemed to me that twenty-six years had passed. He did not know or that the time difference between the two points was eight hours, which had to be added.

"Welcome to Italy. How was the trip?"

They spoke In Italian and I didn't understand what they were saying and confused I looked at the two friends. With a smile then they spoke to me in Spanish:

"This is the language you need to learn urgently, but don't worry that, as we promised you, you're initially going to a school."

Renato lived in the city center, near Piazza del Popolo, next to Villa Borghese, which is a large park in the city of Rome that includes styles other than the garden in Italian to vast areas of English-style buildings, fountains and ponds. It contains numerous buildings, museums and attractions inside.

It was the month of December when I arrived in the city of Rome. It was the middle of winter. the trees were bare, they had no leaves and their branches extended towards the gray sky.

I was amazed and compared to what stave or seeing with my native tropical island, which was always flourishing. It was a new world for me and the joy of the Italians especially for that period, towards the end of the year, was contagious and almost at odds with the antiquity of the buildings.

And it came the last day of December. The end-of-year party was held at Renato's house with the participation of many guests, including people from the cinema, theater and television, journalists and special guests of the high society of Rome.

Renato's obvious intention was to introduce me.

"Meet Alicia, future star of Italian cinema."

Renato's secretary, Carmen, a beautiful young Venezuelan woman, befriended me and was the only one I spoke too Spanish with.

The New Year started as a secretary, waiting for my admission to the acting academy.

"When are you going to enroll me in the Academy?" I asked Maria.

"When will Don Renato decides? For now, he wants you to learn to write."

"What about language school?"

"It's also Don Renato's thing."

I began to see reality; the day's passed and I couldn't wait to start my studies. More than two months had passed since I arrived in Italy and there was still no mention of film studios or language schools. Stavo, at least learns Italian.

One morning, I was sitting in front of the typewriter when I heard Renato's presence behind me. Pensav was either reading what he was writing or writing and not impressed or not at all impressed. Suddenly you hear him grab my hands and kiss me on the neck.

My Eastern Indian blood went up to my head and without thinking I turned away the hands that held me, while I almost screamed in a sharp tone:

"How dare you, disrespect, touch me your lousy old man?"

In the fight, I threw the chair back pushing Renato, but he's very quick, tried to slap me.

"Damn it, you'll see!"

Blinded by his arrogance, I looked around looking for something to defend myself and near me I found a vase full of flowers and without thinking, I threw it at Renato.

"Damn you're going to pay for it!"

Renato bent over avoiding being hit and the only thing he managed to do was wet his clothes with the water and flowers it contained, while the vase crashed against the wall, with so much noise that the girl of herself showed up in the living room.

Renato dismissed her with insults so much that the girl walked away in fear.

I took advantage of that moment to leave the room towards the hallway, but Renato was willing to get what he wanted. He took me back by the arms and pushed me into the room where he threw me on the bed. I fell face down, but as I fell, I noticed that on one side of the bed was a dress hanging from a wooden coat hanger with a hook; I caught him and hit Renato's ribs, causing him to falter. Immediately afterwards I hit him in the stomach. The old man lost his balance and dropped himself against the window, bumping with his head.

"Old worm!"

At that moment I managed to leave the room and, entering the bathroom, I locked and I eased a contrasting chair for greater safety.

"Open Alice to me, please!" pleaded.

Tired of insisting so long, he went to his room, changed his clothes and left the house.

From the bathroom I called the clerk to find out if Renato had already left. Luckily, that was the case. It's not wasting time to call the only person who can give me the information you need: Carmen, the Venezuelan. I asked her on the phone of the Cuban Embassy in Rome and when I had the telephone number I phoned immediately.

Embassy Of Cuba In Rome

An embassy officer didn't take long to arrive, he took me under his arm and took me to talk to the Consul, to whom he tells me what had happened.

"I was assaulted by a man named Renato Spera."

I presented my case to the two members of the Embassy, one of whom said to me:

"(IT) The situation is more serious than that which you imagine because on these days in Europe there is a lot of talk about 'white traffic', that is, an international organization that goes to various countries, especially America, and uses girls deceived with work to do and after sales and Arabs for Muslim harems."

With this in mind and for the fact that Renato had not told me to the Italian authorities to make my presence in Italy legal, they sent the same officer to call him from his home.

When he arrived he was nervous and scared.

First, they questioned him alone and then in my presence, and for the third time he explains how I had come from Cuba, how I had been deceived and finally outraged.

I did not deceive you; I wait for some contacts to apply for immigration permission and start training at the Academy of Dramatic Art in Rome."

"What about the assault? We remind you that the girl is underage."

"It was an unfortunate act on my part, it wasn't my intention to offend you, plus I have permission signed by your father."

This father's permission... certainly not to rape her... and then it is not valid if it has not been reported to the immigration office. The best thing is that it facilitates the return to Cuba.

Renato saw that it was good for him, since, simply by giving the value of the ticket, he had got rid of a tremendous problem and, without much thought, gave in cash the value of the ticket to Cuba.

When Renato Spera left the Embassy, the Consul in a mischievous tone asked me:

"You're actually no longer illegal, now we're going to report you with permission to stay, if that's what you want or want to go back to Cuba?"

I couldn't believe it, I wanted to stay, I wanted to work, she was so eager to become a movie star that I immediately replied: "I want to stay."

Well, we can help you get a job, wait a minute.

"My God! I thought this is a real miracle."

After a few brief phone calls, the Consul procured me a job interview in a fur shop and gave me the money left by Renato. I hugged him and with a satisfied smile the consul fired me, but not before reminding me: "The Embassy of Cuba is like a little piece of your country."

Leave the Embassy happy as if I had achieved a great victory and I thought: "Ora I have control, I am free." I looked at the address that the Consul had given me and stopped a taxi to reach the fur shop.

Rita de la Torre, Conte Vasselli's Italian secretary, once told me that she had left a room in the residential complex where she lived. I called Rita and thankfully the room was still available.

He then started my work in the fur shop, where they appreciated me for the kindness and charisma and with Rita we spoke in Italian until bed time.

On a Saturday afternoon, Rita invited me to visit Depaoli's film studios: Enthusiasm was skyrocketing. Volevor see how the films were made an opportunity that he could not refuse.

Alice Nanditalian Cinema

We arrived at the studios. Rita and I sat in the back of the car and Rita's agent with the driver in the front seats. When we were walking through the entrance to the studios, a black luxury car came in. The man in the other car ordered his driver to report the driver of the car where we were to stop.

A tall, well-dressed man gets out of the car after his driver opens the door for him and turns to Rita's agent and greets him and asks him.

"Who's that girl? I'm looking for a girl like that for my next movie."

The man who got out of the car and is now talking to the agent is tall, of a strong build, is about 30 years old, his eyes are blue and brown hair has soft curls.

Ask her if she wants to work in the cinema.

The agent turned to me to introduce me to the newcomer.

"I'm pleased to introduce you to Doménico Salvi, film producer."

"Great piacere, Alicia Paneque Fuentes."

We had a short conversation. He asked me: where do you live, where do you work? Would you like to work in a movie? He finally gave me a business card with his name, address and phone number.

"I hope to see you tomorrow at 11:00 in my office at this address."

He took my hand and with a gesture of gallantry, kissed me gently, greeted others and headed for his waiting car. I turned to the agent a little incredulous.

"Is it true what he says?"

"Of course, you can go with confidence to tomorrow's appointment."

"Look, Salvi started out as an extra in Cinecittà and overcame all ranks, was the group's leader, actor, production secretary, general organizer and final producer. He has worked with Federico Fellini and Vittorio de Sica, who have just produced Davide and *Goliath and The Terror of barbarians,* with Chelo Alonso and Steve Reeves. I've known him for a long time; he's an honest man you can trust.

In this recommendation, I felt like a lucky woman who really had luck. It was my destiny. Nothing will stop me." I thought. "I'm going to the appointment tomorrow."

The next day, it was a spring morning, I got up happy, I dressed in a very elegant way, as I used to, and went out to meet the producer. I have reason to be glad, Salvi had plans for me. When he arrived at the, there was a production photographer, the screenwriter and the director.

Salvi received me as a movie star. First, he showed me the luxurious office and as he walked down the hallway I looked up at the rooms and the question that came to mind was:

"What century are those chairs?"

"They are in baroque style from the 1400s; the chandelier you just saw at the entrance is made of Bohemian glass."

Then he took me by the arm and pointed me towards a tall, large door that opened into two parts, revealing a vast room, with the same style of antique furniture that filled the entire office.

At the entrance to the living room there were two huge windows that gave a lot of light when the satin curtains opened, antique pink. The floor was made of wood with geometric figures, covered only in two parts by Persian carpets.

I sat on a satin, gilded sofa.

By sliding my hands on the silk of the sofa and placing my head on the upper part of the back, at the same time I asked him:

"What century is this sofa?"

"It's a Louis XV, I see you like antique furniture. When you are the actress, I have in mind to make you become you can buy anything you want … But now I want you to see some people who want to meet you." Then he gave me his hand to help me get up.

We headed for the big door and Salvi said to me:

"You know I was looking for a real name for you last night, and I found it, what do you think about Bella Cortez?"

As he walked, I repeated the name aloud: "Bella Cortez, Bella Cortez, I like it."

I said looking him in the eye and from that moment he adopted it as his name of art.

After taking photos and talking to everyone, Salvi with a movement, almost unreservedly, took from one of his pockets, a bunch of keys and offered them to me.

"Look, this is the key to my suite at the American Palace hotel, which is located in Parioli Avenue. Now you've become an actress and you can't live with me any ragazza. I'm going to stay at my mother's house."

Unbelievable, I couldn't believe it. I felt like I had taken a test and passed it in every way: with the photographer, with the journalists, with the screenwriter and with the production team. I felt like I was renamed because from now on I would be Bella Cortez.

At that moment, the happiest of my life, remember or my childhood in Niquero, my parents and brothers and, unintentionally, remember or even Renato and Vaselli; after all, they were the ones who had taken me to Italy and if it had not been for them now, I would not have had this luck.

I left school with Salvi, went to his house to collect his things and greet his partner and then take possession of the suite he had offered me.

The following days were very happy, Salvi invited me to eat in luxurious restaurants with beautiful views and landscapes of the city of Rome, and we visited luxurious clothing stores and often went to the movies.

"I want you to learn something about acting by watching movies."

This was also an excuse to be close to me, since Domenico Salvi had fallen in love with me, but I'm more than inlove, felt gratitude and a lot of sympathy and nothing more.

Training As An Actress

Doménico did not want to separate from me at any time. He helped me with everything, he took me to the hairdresser, to the production photographer. He introduced me to a choreographer named Leo Coleman who knew how to do his job very well and was excellent at teaching me to dance.

Leo had been a dancer with Katherine Duncan and had participated in choreography for the film *Un Americano in Roma* with Sofía Loren and Cary Grant.

In addition to giving me dance classes and exercises in the morning, we became good friends and since Doménico didn't like to dance, I went to the Night Club accompanied to by Leo, knowing that there was no problem because Leo was gay.

Doménico wanted me to be glamorous in every way, so he bought me a precious fur coat and various jewels. He wanted me to read all the books he brought me and I was as smug and spoiled as I had ever been.

On the other hand, Doménico was preparing the film he wanted me to star in. *The Tartars* starring Orson Welles and Víctor Mature, under the direction of Richard Torpe and worldwide distribution at MGM.

Everything suggested that the film would be a colossus.

As the preparation for the first film was coming to an end, Doménico sold the script to Lux because he needed money to cover some expenses from the previous film. He then assumed the position of general organizer and Prince Tasca as production director.

The film takes place between the Tatars of Mongolia and the Vikings. I was to play the role of the main protagonist among the women, a Tatar princess kidnapped by a young Viking, who forcibly takes her to her fortress, where she remains for a long time and there the love between the two is born.

After a hard battle between the Vikings and the Tatars, to save their princess, peace is restored between the two peoples and lovers leave together on a ship.

With Doménico we traveled to Yugoslavia to choose the places where the filming would take place and to obtain the necessary permits. Taking the train at night in Rome, in gabine read, the next morning we arrived in Trieste, where a car sent by Salvi, the previous morning, was already waiting for us.

When we arrived in Zagreb, we had a beautiful suite at Hotel Splanade and askedfor a fruit basket and a bottle of wine. When the wine arrives, Doménico served it very kindly and offered it to me. He looked at me intensely from top to bottom with desires or and now that he had me so close, while making the toast, he felt the scent emanating from my body and that he himself had given me. Until now Dominic had behaved like a gentleman.

"Let's toast the triumph in your first performance!"

Thank you. I answered him with a smile.

It had been six months since we met and Salvi had never expressed his feelings to me. But at that moment he couldn't resist. The scent of my skin ignited the passion he felt for me and he couldn't take it anymore; he put the glass on the table and drew me to himself, kissing me on the lips, with ardent passion, whispering:

"I want you to be mine, just mine!"

He rested me on the bed and began kissing me from the neck down. I was taken by passion and without saying anything else I gave to him in the honeys of love.

The next morning, we took the car with the driver who had taken us there and headed for a river called Rijeka which is divided into two branches that form an island in the middle. It seemed very suitable for building the Tártari village. We picked up the car and went to Sibenik, near Split, where we found a magnificent place.

Nature seemed to have left things there intact, and seeing all that beauty, the trees and the countryside, it remained the estasiata. Domenico makes me notice the beauty of the lake, where one jet of water falls in the other and each time for me the small waterfall in drops of white foam, which disappears later. The shadows of the trees reflected in the water gave the whole thing a feeling of mystery.

"Look Bella, this is where the Vikings will live."

After analyzing the place, we decided to return to the hotel in Zagreb.

While packing for the return trip to Rome, comment on the beauty of those places.

"How beautiful the place is and what wonderful landscapes."

While I was talking to him, Domenico called on the phone to pick up his luggage. He then reappeared the call, approached me, took me for life and kissed me.

"Yes, the places are as beautiful as you and we will see them very soon so that you always bring me good luck."

He tried to kiss me again, but at that moment came the bellboy for suitcases.

Rome - Railway Station

Doménico and I got off the train and the driver who had or in Yugoslavia came and picked us up.

"How was your trip? Do you know anything about the tests that will be performed tomorrow?"

"It went well thank you, for the tests I inform you that everything is ready for tomorrow at 9:00 at the Di Paoli Theater."

When Doménico arrives at her office, she calls designer Giovanna Del Chiappa (a friend of many years), talks to her, thanks her and then hangs up her phone; on her face there is a mischievous smile, calls the driver and says "Giovanni, go find a package that Mrs. Del Chiappa will give you and bring it to me without opening it."

When he was alone, he told me.

"Tomorrow I have a surprise for you, study the part I gave you and think well that tomorrow is your day!"

"But how can you be so sure if they try other girls?"

"Don't worry, let me do it."

The next morning, I had prepared myself and studied the parts of the characters or Samia. Domenico was more excited and nervous than I was instructing the makeup artist.

"It must look Asian, stretch your eyes with braces."

After the makeup to my surprise, Doménico gives me a Princess Samia costume. It was the dress he had asked

Giovanna del Chiappa. Felice throws with gratitude into Domenico's arms and kisses him on the lips. Then I took one last look in the mirror before going out to the theater where they were already rehearsing.

And where director Richard Torpe was, he looked at me for a long time and noticed that I had (oblique) eyes like the Tartars, a princess crown on my head, and I wore a silk and gold costume. I looked exactly like the character described in the script.

The director, pleased and realizing that there was something between Doménico and me, smiles at both of them and, taking me by the arm, puts me in front of the camera. I behave naturally as if I'm a lifelong man, when other people just seeing a camera makes them nervous.

Richard Torpe begins to try while Doménico went to talk to the cameraman, also friend and pointing at me says:

"Take care, it's okay. Okay?"

It was a good experience to succeed; I passed the tests, signed a ten-week contract and left for Yugoslavia.

Orson Welles

When Orson Welles arrived in Zagreb, Prince Tasca, who was the production director, said to me:

"Try entertaining him by taking a walk around the city."

I knew the city a little bit because I was already with Doménico looking for the locations for the film. Tasca gave me the production machine, driven by Giovanni. So, I thought I'd show Welles the Tatar fortress and take it to the Rijeka River.

To reach the other part where, for mysterious reasons of nature, the river opened leaving an island in the middle, you would take a rowboat. So, we got off the boat and started walking.

Look at that big house in the middle, that's where your character will live. - I told him. And then, we walked to the house and when we reached the portal, I asked Orson

"What's behind that door?"

Orson climbed the steps, inviting me to climb, and when we were on top, he opened the door. As is natural in all or almost every building in the cinema, there was nothing behind those walls of tree trunks, so he held out his hand so that I could get off after him, but he took me towards him and tried to kiss me.

He had strength in his sturdy arms but I was agile and with a circular movement I freed him and slapped him.

And in that moment of confusion, I ran without stopping on the boat, went up and crossed the river leaving Orson on the other side. Still agitated by the ride I reached the car and told the driver.

"I left it on the other side..."

John did not ask any questions and run towards the boat.

On the way back to the hotel nothing was said, John occasionally glanced at the rearview mirror, but that was it. At night Orson calls me on the phone to apologize for his behavior and I forgive him.

Because you forgave me, I invite you to dinner.

"Ok accetto."

After hanging up the phone I am thoughtful and decide either to invite my closest colleagues and proceed to draw up a list of eleven people; call them or all and prendor an appointment at19:00 in the waiting room. When he called them, he told each one.

"You're invited to dinner tonight, Orson Welles pays!"

Already prepared and well dressed, I sat in a room armchair with my legs pinned and my back thrown backwards in a relaxed position, my face immersed in the light of the bedside lamp, I discovered in me a certain humor. I read the script to entertain a little bit and looked at my wristwatch, and I was mischievously laughing.

Eventually the phone rang; I became serious and cleared my voice before answering "Hey!"

It was Leo Escucugbia, the group's interpreter, sent by Orson and complicit in what I was up to.

We're all here, you can come down.

I give him the last instructions and hung up the phone, took the evening bag that was on the bed and left the room.

When he went down to the lobby, with a surprised face, I began to greet all the guests and ask them:

"Where are you going?"

"Dinner naturally!"

"Coincidentally, I'm also going to dinner with Orson Welles."

"There's no way we're going to separate now. Come."

After a brief introduction, and to Orson's surprise; the group exits to pick up their respective vehicles. Some of them had taken their cars from Italy and others by taxi, while Orson and I had the production machine at our disposal with Leo acting as an interpreter.

The journey was short and when I got down in front of the restaurant Orson held out my hand to get out of the car whispering:

"What's going on?"

Nothing, don't worry.

They all walked into the restaurant and here they were sitting at the table, Orson sitting at the table head, looked and counted the seated people, including himself, realized that there were thirteen of us (an unfortunate number), then invited the waiter who was serving them to sit with them.

"Thank you, Sir. But I'm forbidden to do what you ask me to do."

At Orson's insistence, the waiter got nervous, confused by what he was doing. The nervousness was so great that he poured a fish with mayonnaise on Orson's dress.

"Excuse me, sir, that's too bad!"

So he immediately proceeded to clean the blue jacket that Orson was wearing and he didn't say a single word, he seemed very nervous- but without losing his diplomacy. He looked at me and I tried to hide my smile by putting a hand on my nose.

Then I comforted him: "Don't worry; you don't see the stain anymore."

After the accident and after dinner, everyone agreed that it was too early to go to sleep and Leo had the idea to go to the Esplanade Hotel Night Club where everyone was staying. The idea seemed good and they asked for the bill, when he arrived, they passed it to Orson as if it were a hot potato, looked at it, asked for a pen, signed it and gave it to the waiter.

"Send it to Lux Productions who will pay for it."

That said, he got up from the table, held out his hand to help me, taking me by the arm. Once we arrived at the hotel, we heard the music playing and the faces were happy, looking at each other.

The night club was small but cozy, decorated with lights of various colors and decorative plants, even the tables were small to make room on the dance floor.

When we arrived, we sat by a high window that didn't face the street, but a hallway that in turn gave access to the hotel restaurant, the exterior window had a few floors so passers-by couldn't look in.

Orson called the waiter and asked for wine; with that the drink, and with that toast he would have liked to erase the bad start that was created between them. At that time the orchestra played something sweet and romantic to dance.

The next morning, Prince Tasca showed up in the hotel lobby, visibly nervous about the prank on the restaurant bill.

After splitting the sum, he wrote on the hotel board what each one had to pay, with a note that said: "If it happens again, you will be fined each. Tomorrow at 6:00 am they will start filming the film; the whole company should be in the lobby at that time."

It was time to start, first with the interns and then with the extras, but the whole crew wanted to see Orson Welles meet Victor Mature because it was known that there was an old quarrel between the two because of the famous actress Rita Hayworth, many years ago.

The crew's hopes of seeing a fight between the two famous Hollywood actors fell apart when Victor entered the theater looking at everything and realized that Orson was there too.

With his hands behind his back, looking up, as if admiring the columns of the palace, walking and turning until he collided back-to-back with Orson who also pretended and looked towards the throne, he turned his back on Victor.

In the end they collided and as springs they both turned around and, to everyone's surprise, greeted each other like a couple of compatriots who are in distant lands and began to talk as if nothing had happened between them.

I was a little late, and Orson introduced me to Victor.

"I'm Víctor Mature, to serve you. It is nice to meet you, Bella Cortez."

After the presentation they left together for makeup.

While Orson does his own makeup, I see the actor's transformation into an Asian; it's like he's someone else. The creativity that is inside him begins to emerge and I realize, day after day, how demanding he is, so much so that he wants to change the part that corresponds to him in the script, and also direct his scenes also changing the costumes that Giovanna del Chiappa has designed for him.

When these things reached Víctor Mature's ears, he also began to change costumes and invited a Hollywood writer to rewrite his scenes because he is not like Orson, who knows how to write and direct but does not want to be left behind. Along with the writer came a box of whiskey because Victor liked to drink his drinks, which he did not hide.

Jealousy begins again between the two Hollywood stars, to the point that the stopwatch has been used to measure the seconds of the close-ups, thus exposing itself to the comments and mockery of the crew.

As far as I'm concerned, director Richard Torpe has also changed the costumes for me. He took a slave robe, gave it to the film's seamstress so that it could be arranged according to my measurements. The woman refused because she was friends with Giovanna and did not want to compromise, so Torpe took the scissors himself and made a large number of cuts to the vest and, he grabbed a leather belt and gave it to me for the costume I would use during almost all the shooting.

Very soon the news of what was happening arrived in Rome and the company of Rugero Peruzzi and Giovanna del Chiappa filed a lawsuit for abuse of Lux production. At first what appeared to be a Colossal movie was slowly collapsing.

In one scene in the Tatar fortress, I was kidnapped by a young Viking and taken on horseback, but we had to cross a burning gate. The horse went out of his mind, got up on two legs and nagged. When he put his feet back in front of the ground, he flew forward over the horse's head, hitting a leg against the crossbar of the gate, but did not let his composure. I had the agility to prevent the horse from trampling on me.

Prince Tasca and actor Luciano Marín, who played the young Viking, immediately came to lift me off the ground and took me to the trailer. Seeing that they could not film with me because of the great pain in my leg, they transported me to the hotel and called the doctor, not knowing that the doctors were not visiting that country.

Considering the wound and pain in my leg, I was transported to the hospital where I was ordered to do an X-ray to detect any fractures. Journalists found out and the news reached Rome.

In the morning, Domenico was reading the newspaper and learned of the incident, immediately called Yugoslavia to find out from me what the seriousness of the matter was.

"Dimmi Bella what happened?"

"I just have to rest for a week while the swelling passes."

Thus, taking advantage of the call, dissi:

"Why don't you come to Sibenik? We're moving in next week and I'd love to see you!"

Domenico, who I already missed, replied: "Yes my love, I will come."

The following week I was packing my bags to leave for Sibenik, when I received a call from prince, production manager.

"Hi Bella, is there any problem traveling with Luciano Marín in his car, so he doesn't go alone?"

"No problem, don't worry, I'm going with Luciano."

I started thinking, "What can happen? He is a young man married with a small child, and I am doing a favor to the production and then he is friends with Domenico."

I had no idea that everything had been planned by Luciano to be alone with me. Swings in the car, when they drove away from the city of Zagrebon the road that skirted a mountain, the caravan of cars and trucks went up and down, disappearing from view and reappearing.

Luciano was letting the cars pass one by one, until he was last in the trailer and I slowly decelerate to get away and stay even further behind.

I, who did not know his intentions, ask him:

"Aren't you far behind? Do you know the way to Sibenik?"

"Don't worry, I know the road, and also, look here I have a road map."

Suddenly he stopped the car on the left side of the road. I started getting more and more nervous and angry at him and I said, "And now you're going to stop too? We're going to be late."

"Just a moment to look at the view!"

The road was surrounded by mountains, with a precipice on the right side of the car. I told Domenico that at that time he should have been at the hotel, where they would stay, as agreed.

As he thought about it with his arms folded and the sweater, he was wearing over his shoulders, I felt a slight frost from the air blowing and looking at the across the street. It was the surprises when Luciano took me by the shoulders and said:

"Why are you avoiding me? Any woman would be happy just to travel in my car."

I felt the vanity with which he spoke and angry that he was or delaying, I felt the blood boiling in my veins and with a sudden movement slid to the streets. Luciano took me again by the arms and tried to kiss me. defended him by hitting him on the head and shoulders and when he tried to kiss me, I turn to his head and smear his cheek with lipstick.

"I like you, don't be hard..."

I replied, "Never! You're going to pay me!"

I looked hoping someone was coming by car or on foot and, like a wild cat; I struggled with the attacker furiously. I used to detach it from his arms and, with his free hand, pressed him by the head, pulling his hair and nailing it with his nails on his ear.

Seeing that he wasn't getting what he wanted, the famous actor paused and almost contemptuously, gradually settling into his position, passing a hand in his hair that he had or ruffled and touching his ear to see if he was bleeding. Avevor opened the door with the attempt to escape and did not waste time. Immediately jump out of the car, grab the sweater and start walking.

I did not know where to go, but I knew or that I had to walk, escape from that petty and arrogant man who, he would pay dearly with Domenico.

When Luciano saw me drive away without looking back, he turned on the engine of the car and reached me. Then things turned upside down, now it was Luciano who wanted me to get in the car and almost begged me, while he was or walking. Soon it was the forced to take off my shoes and carry them in one hand because the heels did not help me to walk that path of collina.

As the asphalt ripped off my stockings, I kept walking and Luciano walked next to me in the car.

"Don't you tell me anymore, what are we going to be late for?"

Hearing these words, I stop at and remarry:

"Of course, because Dominico Salvi is waiting for me to go to lunch."

Luciano could not believe it; he knew the producer and knew that Salvi, so dedicated to work, was not the kind of enamor to fall so easily and not such a young girl.

"I can't believe it..."

He opened his eyes and looked up at the sky.

"Get in the car, I promise I won't touch you again, but please don't lie to me, hey, Lord Salvi's in Rome."

He looks at him with a half-smiled mockingly.

"I go up because I don't want to be late to the date with my boyfriend." I told him by showing the shine ring.

"Domenico gave it to me and if you don't believe me ask him when we get there."

I got in the car without losing sight of the actor who started to get rid of the wheels as if trying to free his anger for not being able to realize his attempt and, in turn, to frighten me while I clung to the car handle. Every time a bend approached, it went to the side and my long hair - moved by the wind- coming out of the window from the ruined car gave me.

The impression that I had was some kind of scared doll but I was strong. I promised not to show fear and to say anything. We finally arrived in Sibenik and met Doménico in the hotel restaurant. The two walls were sliding glass doors that revealed a terrace adorned with terracotta vases with geraniums and jasmine; beyond the terrace you could see the valley until the mountains that surrounded it emerged.

Sitting at the table, I had gestures made Domenico understand why he was late and pointing to my face, hair and socks.

Doménico took my hand

"Fear nothing, I'm here now and I'm going to settle the scores with Señorito Marín."

At that moment Luciano entered through the glass door which was right in front of the table were

Doménico was seated, his blue eyes were as cold as ice and piercing like a knife then he tried to hide his surprise because he was convinced that he told him a lie. He smiles in greeting and what comes out is a grimace, then he extends his hand to Doménico, who does not even answer him, and with his eyes fixed on Luciano, he tells me:

"Stay here, I'm coming back now!"

Doménico gets up very quickly passing behind me and taking Luciano by the arm says:

"Come out, we need to talk."

Luciano pales, his face shows how scared he is, and protests.

"What did I do... leave my arm."

I was alone at the table; Leo came to join me and could not help but listen to the discussion when he passed by the two men.

"What's going on?" asked Leo

"I had problems with Marín." I answer without giving details.

"Tell Doménico I went to the bathroom to get ready, see how Marín reduced me."

I was worried about what Doménico would suffer from Luciano, being smaller in stature and thinner in size. Doménico was the first to speak:

"This is going to be the last movie you're going to make with me. If you don't leave Bella alone, I'il ruin your face forever, do you understand me?"

He pointed his finger at his face to keep saying:

"I'm not going to touch you now because you have to keep the movie going, but I'm going to leave you this souvenir."

So, he punched him in the stomach that left him breathless, then turned around, turned his back and walked up to our table.

Several days later (Doménico had gone to Rome) in an external part of the filming of the Battle of the Vikings against theTatars, we were on hiatus because they had to change the cameras. We were sitting next to Victor Mature doing makeup and I was talking to Leo.

"Well, I have little left to finish my part in this film, it was an unforgettable experience, but I miss Rome, my home and above all Doménico."

I stopped to keep saying:

"I think I'm going to go to the doctor in Rome to show him my throat because it hurts a little bit, with all this dust that horses lift."

Leo was responding to him when Victor Mature called him insistently pointing out to him with his hand that he wanted to talk to me, but he didn't have to wait and insisted again. Leo with a negative or head movement, hinted at me.

"Let me go see what's going on, so he'll leave us alone."

As Leo approaches Victor, he rests his elbow on his thigh and his hand on his face, he tells Leo as a secret:

"Tell Bella I want to marry her and take her to Hollywood with me!"

"Don't play with Bella with these things." Leo replied.

Victor then, settling back in his chair, replied "And who's playing? Go tell him."

Leo looks at him in disbelief, calls me and says: - Come and hear what Victor proposes to you. -

I approached, Leo did the translation and I replied:

"Ask him if he thinks I'm stupid at? First: I know he's waiting for the wife who came when he asked the writer and the whiskey boxes."

"When Leo finished translating, Victor replied: "It doesn't matter, divorce!"

I understood without Leo having to do the translation and then concluded:

Secondly, he's very old for me and third: I'd never marry a man who drinks as much liquor as he does.

Leo didn't know how to tell Victor what I had just said and it occurred to him to just say:

Bella said no.

Victor, who had something to drink in a thermos and no one knew what it was, took a drink and answered

"With everything you talked about, you didn't say anything else?"

In what they call him to experience the scene where, Victor finds his character's wife more on the ground and me who was sitting in a Viking or two-wheeled wagon, while Victor tried to cover the center of his head with his huge hands so that the baldness, he was advancing was not seen filming the scene of grief over his wife's death. So, I thought,

"The vanity of this actor who's already in decline, he's so big, he doesn't mind ruining the scene to look good."

The film was still being made when I finished my part and I was happy to be free from commitments and to be able to go back to what he called my free land. Free from Cuban communism, which throughout the world echoed what Fidel Castro did with Cuba and the Cubans and free from Yugoslav socialism.

Error happy to have finished my first movie, with some setbacks but I had done it. It couldn't be removed from my resume. All thanks to Doménico Salvi.

With those thoughts in my mind, he went to Trieste to catch the train that would take me to Rome.

I wasn't traveling by plane because I was very young then and he was scared. Rhymes to leave calls the Doménico.

"I'm leaving this afternoon, arriving in Rome in the morning."

Well, honey, I have a surprise for you when you're here.

Domenico's House

When I arrived in Rome, I found the surprise that Domenico had told me about the night before on the phone. He no longer lived in the suite of the Hotel Parioli, but had rented an apartment for us and was waiting for me to come back to arrange the furniture and make it beautiful with decorations.

The apartment was less large than the suite but more intimate and welcoming; it was the first step Doménico took to live with me. I felt or protected by him because he pampered me and favored me in everything he wanted or, so when he wanted or the furniture, he had in his office room, he said nothing but this:

"I don't need to have such a big office; even that room is almost no longer used."

The décor of the living room consisted of a sofa covered with an ancient species of pink silk, with their armchairs of the same color. Next to the sofa stood two small tables with their respective lamps with an angel-shaped bronze base from the 1800s, such as the white and gold Venetian, hand-painted, which stood on the back wall of the office?

On the other wall was the gold Louis XVI sofa, with its well-shaped and tall legs that gave it a majestic touch. I liked it and it was on that sofa that I already sat or on the first date with Doménico.

All the furniture was transported but the apartment wasn't big enough for much furniture and I felt or uncomfortable not being able to use them, but since he would move to a smaller office, he said to me:

"Anything you want in the furniture, you can take them, except the desks."

There were also baroque chairs from the 1400s, an entrance mirror with its three-legged wall table and a white marble base, Persiancarpets, and Bohemian glass ceiling panels.

But Doménico, nothing can adapt anymore.

"Don't worry, it's not just to decorate the house, it's that I don't want to lose this furniture that costs so much and also has a sentimental value for me."

Listen carefully and reflect.

If at that moment Avessi knew that I would lose Doménico and that over the years even the antique furniture and jewelry he had given me, I did not worry so much.

But now it's just listening to the past that I go back to, without regretting anything. And I listened again to Domenico's voice that said to me:

"We're moving to a better apartment later, you'll see."

I kept looking at him with a questioning look. Then he took my hand and spoke to me slowly, as if he didn't want anyone to listen.

I need to talk to you; since you went to work in Yugoslavia, things haven't gone as well as I would have liked. The creditors of the film *"The Terror of Barbarians"*are threatening to take off my shirt as well. I calmed them down because they know I'm preparing another movie for this spring, which will be called "The 7 Challenges" and you'll be the protagonist along with Ed Fury.

I looked at him with surprise and admiration and asked:

"Is it another movie? I can't believe it, if my sister Cari saw me..."

He came up to me and putting his hands on my face he said:

"I don't want to sadden my love; everything will be done to save the furniture."

He tried to kiss me, but he put his hands on his throat and feci a grimace.

"Since I was in Yugoslavia, I've had a bad sore throat and now that winter is coming, I've gotten worse at."

Without wasting time, Doménico called Dr. Saladin, his friend, to ask for an appointment and the doctor told him that he would see me immediately.

The doctor, when he examined me, said "Here you need to operate and the faster, the better, because very often you would get sick and have a fever."

Doménico looked at me and concluded:

"If you want to have surgery now, I'm going to pay a person to take care of you and then you'll be fine when the movie starts."

I felt so bad that he said yes, but I asked the doctor.

How long will it take?

Not much, it's going to be fast.

The operation did not take long and once it was over, after recovering from anesthesia I received a good ice cream.

We finally came home and hired a lady named Liliana Molteni, who came every day and gave me liquid food for a fortnight, which made me lose weight. As soon as I got well and I went to the hairdresser, I cut my hair a little, because I wanted to look different, not knowing that some scenes from the movie "The Tartars" had gone wrong and I should have done them again on the beach of Rome. When director Richard Thorpe saw me so changed, he ordered me to wear a wig similar to how I had hair before, but nothing could be done because of the weight. It seemed fatally that the film's problems didn't end. When it was made public, the film went unnoticed. It was a failure.

Return To Zagreb

In April 1961 I was called upon to shoot the film *The Seven Challenges* in Yugoslavia, with Ed Fury and Elaine Stewart, directed by Primo Seglio; Doménico was the executive producer.

I remember that at that time the snow was still falling in Zagreb and since he had only seen it in movies and magazines, I did not wait for or touch it with my own hands. I liked to see how it piled up on the edge of the sidewalks, on top of cars and on leafless trees, covered only in that soft white snow.

One morning when I woke up at the airs at the window and saw the snowing and I went out without thinking of covering myself very much or covering my feet well. I had high heels and thin soles, very happy just to have left my room and leave the Esplanade Hotel.

"Ah … Delicious!"

The first breath of cold air struck my face still calda; lift to the lapel of the coat and put my hands on my throat to protect me.

I started walking and walked the rather steep road. When I was almost downhill, near the sidewalk, the fresh snow wet my shoes and the slope of the descent made me accelerate my pace and gradually press the speeds until it slipped to and fell, hitting the ground with my butt.

The fall surprised me, but it was the most surprising of pain in the last vertebra of the spine. The cold made me rise quickly because the stockings and coat were wet. I looked everywhere to see if anyone was looking at me. I shrugged off the snow covering my coat and with a deep sigh you start climbing the driveway to get into the hotel again.

The same day, after talking to Doménico on the phone and reporting to him what had happened to me, but before he arrived, he met some of the men in the company.

"We're going to surprise Bella by giving her a baptism of snow." I heard.

Then they advanced towards me with a mischievous smile and with their hands behind. Furio Meniconi spoke:

"So, this is the first time you're seen snow, huh?"

And they threw the snowballs, but to their surprise I ran where there was enough snow piled up, grabbed it with both hands and reacted to the attackers by hitting them too who laughed. We had fun that day and took a lot of pictures.

The film was over and Domenico and I returned to Rome, while the house full of furniture was waiting for us. We started to see the possibility of moving into a larger apartment and after seeing the different, we decided on one of four rooms. I didn't feel or more oppressed by so much furniture, now I thought or to decorate everything and fix them where there was enough space.

One night while I was asleep, I woke up sweating and with intense pain on the right side of the ovaes. Trying to go back to sleep but can't make it or more.

"Domennico!"

"What's wrong, Bella?"

"I have a lot of pain, call Dr. Saladin."

It was four in the morning when the doctor arrived and he found out it was serious. Avevor an inflammation in the appendix had affected me landova. They immediately took me to the hospital and operated on me as a matter of urgency. The operation ended well and when I wake up to the, the first thing I saw was Doménico, who were there with his brother, a bouquet of flowers and some magazines to entertain me while he was in the hospital.

It was the end of May and, as soon as I recovered, Doménico showed me the script of the new film he intended to make: *The Giant of Metropolis* with Gordon Mitchell, Roldano Lupi, directed by Umberto Scarpelli.

The plot of the film was good; it was about a bad king who discovered a formula to keep his father alive for 200 years, giving him a brain of superior intelligence.

His father already tired of living and feeling like a human experiment, however, tells him.

"Oh, my son, all right, I want to die!"

In response, the mad king imprisons him with the intention of transplanting his father's brain to his nine-year-old son. Suddenly it appears, carried by the waves of the sea, a good giant full of muscles. The king's daughter finds him and hides him from the guards so that his father does not know. When he discovers that the giant has supernatural strength, he asks him to save his younger brother from certain death if his father has given him the intended transplant.

The giant fights with the guardians of the evil king, manages to defeat them and save the boy. After the battle there is an explosion in the submerged city and the only survivors are Mesedes, the giant and the boy. Mesedes and this is the character I should have played.

Filming began early and, soon, I befriended Gordon Mitchell, the lead actor, and Liana Orfei, with whom I had already worked on the first film with Orson Welles. Liana plays the mad king's favorite, but is killed by him with her sword when she opposes the brain transplant to Mesedes' younger brother. **FOR THE MOVIE: ANY SCENES TAKEN FROM THE GIANT OF METROPOLIS**

Gordon was born in North America and had moved to Italy to play the main character; he studied psychology and the physical culture he practices assiduously obtaining an athletic body, well-formed and really full of muscles.

During filming came the month of December and the sixteenth was my birthday. That afternoon, Domenico told the company staff to take a break, ordered me to remove the costume he was wearing or to wear personal clothes.

I thought it was a break for the completion of a set, but no, in the studio there was a table with flowers, sweets and gifts. Everyone who worked with Doménico was aware of the birthday but had said nothing to make it a real surprise.

The stage photographer was hidden to take the photos suddenly and capture the impression of my face. Doménico went looking for me to enter the studio together and when we did, everyone, men and women, suddenly appeared shouting: - Surprise!!! -

Among other things they gave me a bohemian glass vase full of red roses. This vase accompanied me for many years.

Once the interns were finished in the studio, the entire crew moved to Naples, near Vesuvius, where they filmed part of the volcano where Mesedes finds the giant. It was an exceptional experience.

On that occasion I visited the city of Pompeii with its sad museum of people mummified by lava that had surprised them by sleeping and still seem intact today.

Everything around them was covered with grayish stones. The earth, after the fall of the lava of the volcano, had turned into a hard stone and stone. Since then, nothing has been growing in the surroundings and there are kilometers of wasteland while Vesuvius was active.

The city of Naples was very picturesque. At night we went for walks and dined in restaurants on the Tyrrhenian shore. Salvi would tip the players to make them sing for me that I was happy.

Before leaving Naples, we visited the islands of Ischia and Caprí, wonderful places that fascinate any tourist, walking through the streets and shops and buying some souvenirs to take to Rome.

Filming ended and was turned to Rome. Avevor all but felt, or certain loneliness and it had been a long time since I had seen my relatives. So, talk to Domenico:

Doménico, I want to know your opinion on the possibility of inviting my sister Caridad home.

"Okay, you can do it, so you'll be in good company."

For the month of September, when the filming of "*Vulcan Son of Jupiter* "began, Caridad's arrival in Rome was decided. There had been no visit and since December 1959.

I went to meet her at the airport and was very happy when I saw her, because despite the mistreatment received by Caridad, during the seven years I had lived with her, I had no grudge, on the contrary I wanted to share with my sister some of the well-being and happiness that then surrounded me.

I offered her the empty room and Domenico got her a butler. This was a former Franciscan priest who, sent to Africa as a missionary, due to a scandal in which he was involved because he was gay, had removed him from the Franciscan order. In Rome he met Salvi, whom he asked and worked as a butler. Everything has a beginning and an end and now something is happening between me and Doménico. For several months he had not had more had sex, we had become, to say the least, as a father and daughter or 1 brother or sister.

I didn't know then that Salvi had a lot of financial problems, and he didn't inform me not to worry. He also feared going to prison for signing fake checks to his creditors for films previously made as a producer. So, he just thought about making more movies using my name to sell them and then pay some of his creditors.

On the other hand, I didn't care much about abstinence, error just had surgery and the less it touched me, the better it was for me and also because, with the start of filming for the last film, I met Yoohyeh Khoshabeh's actor, weightlifting champion, winner of the 1957 Mr. Universe title. He had received 46 tournament cups and 11 national and international medals in the past, but the most important thing was that love was born at first sight.

However, we both knew either that it was dangerous and that he was playing with fire.

Yoohyeh asked his theatrical agent:

"Bella has someone particularly interested in her?" And he replied:

"Bella lives with Doménico Salvi, who is the producer of the film we are making."

"Devils!"

But it didn't matter much, my youthful beauty and desire to kiss me, they burned his skin and when we shot the love scenes, the whole company noticed.

"They love each other." They were ensavano, but no one said anything, much less to their employer so as not to hurt him. They were people who had been working with Salvi for many years and knew his feelings and sensitivity.

A wardrobe warden, who took care of the costumes and had confidence in me, came up to me and said: "Look what you do, because everyone knows you love it."

After a short time, I called Yoohyeh and sadly said to him:

"I don't want Doménico to suffer for our love."

I stopped, thinking about what I had said, and I continued.

"Also, nothing happened between us other than the scenes of the film, so we avoid comments among the production companions." **FOR THE FILM ANY SCENES FROM VOLCANO SON OF JUPITER**

Yet fate would have decided otherwise. That afternoon, when filming ended, we exchanged phone numbers and then called to go to his house, with my sister, to a dinner he prepared, Persian style.

A Dinner At Yoohyeh's House

Dinner day came. I went with my sister Caridad to the actor's apartment a date Lamb Chiscabab with white rice, salad, fresh fruit and wine and, finally, we went into the living room with a glass of cognac that put me in a state of Sana intoxication, relaxed and joyful than ever before.

Time passed and without noticing. Caridad, for his part, seeing that he was getting late, told me that he wanted to leave but I felt or so well next to that strong, muscular man, with a deep and veiled voice and a beautiful smile with his white and uniform teeth.

I really liked his tanned, soft skin that I had felt when he ate and he had stroked my legs under the table, that's why I said to Caridad:

"Go away, Dears, if you will; we have to study tomorrow's scripts."

We understand for a fact that the 1957 Mr. Universe was the great Arthur Robin. He is currently 93 years old.

My sister left with the driver, very worried because she understood that we liked him and wondered:

"What if Doménico realizes that my sister is in love with the lead actor? And what will happen to Bella's career?"

When Charidad left the apartment, neither resisted the wish and we hugged each other, as if to say:

"Finally, alone, my love." Without saying anything.

We stopped for just one moment until the mouths were searched and we kissed with a passion that had been brooding for months and that they could no longer repress. The love then came sudden and tender and we did nothing to resist, controlling it.

"I want you to know that I don't give up on such a weak woman in my Muslim religion when we really want to love are for life and I want to marry you."

I kissed him passionately.

Then show me that you give you to me because you want to marry me. -

We walked hugged towards the bedroom and the door closed behind us. We made love more passionate, where the whole or world shuddered when we reached the pinnacle. It was sex as only two lovers can do, then I fell asleep in his arms.

The sound of the phone woke me up, it was Caridad.

"I remind you that Doménico is about to return home."

I hung up the phone, put on my vestii and kissed the Yoohyeh.

"See you tomorrow onset."

After that afternoon, we saw each other very often, in the gym, at home, even on the set where they were trying to be together. We called on the phone, we were looking for each other, and we couldn't be without each other anymore.

The film ended and Doménico was still around with the creditors, to the point that he decided to go a few days to Abruz zo where his parents had a house and hide until his mind was free to start again.

I Had Been Left Alone, And I Took The Opportunity To Consolidate Hidden Love And Study A Script That Doménico Had Brought Me For A Comedy Film Entitled

"Hot Day At Paradise Show" With Nino Taranto, Memo Carotenuto, Tiberio Murgia And The Musical Casting Of Nini Rosso, Peppino Di Capri, Nunzio Gallo And Little Tony, With The Ballet By Dimitri Costgantinov And Directed By Enzo Digianni. Scenes From The Film

I liked working, that's why I accepted everything Domenico brought me, but I never asked him what he did with my money. Or I didn't miss anything. I had jewelry, a well-stocked wardrobe of clothes, home, vehicle and driver available only by calling the production.

The film ended, almost at the end of the year.

For Christmas of that year, 1962, I bought a Christmas tree and, together with my sister, we arranged it in a corner of the room, near the large window that opened onto the terrace where I lulled myself into a hammock to contemplate it. That year we celebrated Christmas with roast turkey. The end-of-year festivities came and went, with the same tradition, eating grapes at twelve in the evening and taking some good shots of Cuban rum.

Doménico, he worked hard to find work for me, and so he raised money to pay his debts.

In May 1963, filming began on *The King of Brute Force*, directed by Antonio Leonviola and distributed by Warner Brothers. The film was shot in Yugoslavia, in the caves of Postumia, where humidity and cold, make the work more difficult than it actually was. **SCENES FROM THE FILM**

It was interesting to see the wonders that nature cando. The caves intertwine until they are out of sight between stalactites and stalagmite everywhere. A fascinating thing is how, drop by drop, they have formed and, over thousands of years, any and thinner than a strand of hair and all the different colors of the minerals they contain.

Nature can be very beautiful, but that place is scary and chilling, especially due to a precipice that has a river at the bottom, so deep that if you throw a rock, you can't hear it fall until after at least 30seconds.

In early 1963, before going to Yugoslavia, he began a film called "The Seven Labors of *Ali Baba*" *con* RodFlash Yoohyeh, this is the name Doménico gave Yoohyeh to make him remember and pronounce more easily. He was directed by himself and, in those shoots, I had a small accident, in my back.

In a scene where I danced an Arabic dance, I had to go out through a hole. Two dancers were responsible for holding me and pulling me back and forth, but they failed and dropped me.

News of the incident spread and journalists came home to interview me about the film and the incident.

With this Ali Baba film, Yoohyeh's work ended. It was never known if Doménico had discovered anything or if it was for another reason. The point was that we kept getting more and more in love. In May, when I traveled to Yugoslavia for Antonio Leonviola's film, I was not very happy because I had left my love in Rome.

I was consoled by the idea that I was not alone, because I was always with my sister Caridad, and that when Yoohyeh left me a turquoise ring with a bright one in the center, as a symbol of the love that we had. In May, when I was in Yugoslavia, Yoohyeh had brought his engagement rings from his country. He was talking about marrying us and having a little girl who looked like me. Apparently, everything was planned between us.

When filming of "Taur the *King of Brute Force*" ended, I immediately returned to Rome, doing what I had planned to do. I realized that Doménico was shamelessly exploiting me, so I went to Fillipo Fortini's theatre agency (Goofy)to get a job and take care of raising my money when I wasn't in Rome.

Goofy took care of my advertising, held a meeting with me inviting Chiara Samugueo, famous photographer of Tempo *magazine,* where a photo interview appeared on two pages. Later I received the Le Ali *D'oroaward, for* his contribution to Italian cinema, on the island of Ischia, making the journey from Naples with Alan Delón and Anna Magnani.

Later I received the *Porsenna award together* with Claudia Cardinale and other well-known actors and actresses. I was happy on that side, I finally saw the results of so much work, even though, until then, I hadn't seen a penny, but I didn't miss anything. If I needed anything, whether it was a dress or a leather for the awards parties, Doménico would give me the money without any problem. He knew the more advertising I received, the more he became a famous to and the better his films were sold.

I received a telegram informing me that he had been nominated for the CiakD'Oro award in Monte Catini for the film *Le Sette Totiche by Ali Baba.* Immediately go to the dalle Sorelle Fontana and buy an exclusive dress and mink fur. At the awards ceremony it was Yoohyeh with his agent Persian Samani and all the photographers who knew me.

And now I see myself again and the past becomes present...

The awards ceremony has begun and all the nominees have been called, leaving me as the last, which makes me nervous and I don't even go out to speak to the microphone because the emotion has invaded me and tears flow down my cheeks. Outside the windows, you can see the fireworks exploding in a thousand colors illuminating the night.

For a few seconds I went even further with my thoughts...

"Who would have imagined, as a child, when I lived with my sister in Cuba..."

And I kept thinking about the mistreatment I had or received.

"Every morning I'd make him coffee and take him to bed, until a day or I burned myself. I cried looking up at the sky and wishing my mother."

And followed the storm of bad memories,

"I remembered how my brother-in-law once hit me because I wasn't washing something he wanted, and how at the age of eleven I cooked and washed my brothers' clothes by hand, and when I was thirteen, "I was thrown out of the house because he couldn't take it anymore."

While I was prey to these bad memories came a photographer, who spoke to me:

"Bella, Bella, what are you doing? Instead of being happy, do you start crying? I smile, I'll take a picture of you with actor Yoohyeh."

All the friends, known and unknown came to the table to congratulate me on the prize received and, on the sensitivity, revealed in my plan.

In June, Pippo Fortini proposed to make a film with actor Christopher Lee and Giorgio Ardison, entitled Katarsis. When I accepted, filming began immediately and while I was working on it, Doménico proposed another one that he would direct: *F.B.I. Call Istanbul,* turkey with actor Ken Clark. **ANY SCENES FROM THE MOVIES.** Of course, I would have been the lead actress to be able to sell the film in Arab countries, where it is well known for the films with Yoohyeh.

While all this was happening, Caridad had planned to return to Cuba to her husband, who she hadn't seen in more than a year.

I told Caridad the money for the trip, for her expenses and to buy Felix what she had asked for, but that wasn't enough for her. At night, when everyone was having sleep, he would stand on tiptoe and put his hands in the pockets of Doménico's pants, until he suspected it; he began counting the money before going to bed.

"Go buy the ticket back to Cuba, the sooner, the better!" I told her.

I noticed that some jewels were missing and I verified that it was Charity and not the service staff who had taken them. What a pity... to think that I had forgiven her for all the abuse to which she had subjected me as a child, avev or brought her to live in my house, she trusted me and from now on embarrassed me with Doménico in that way.

Caridad left, but the ticket was from pan-am airline, and when they saw that he was going to Cuba, a communist country, I was subjected to along interrogation and they brought her back to Rome. At the airport, Caridad called me.

Hey, Bella, how are you?

"Hi Dears, how was the trip?"

"No Bella, I'm in Fiumicino, here at Rome airport, come and see me."

In the end, I went to the airport, after talking to Caridad, and the Pan-Am office to ask for the return of the ticket, because it was the airline's responsibility. He finally reached an agreement on a flight to Budapest and then, via Czechoslovakia, arrived in Cuba.

So, I decided to go on holiday, i don't accept any work because I felt nervous and tired. I was dedicated to exercise and at night, especially on Fridays, and avs or dancing with Leo. On the other hand, she could not be seen with Yoohyeh, who for obvious reasons and for how much she wanted to work, could not, among other things, because she was very demanding in the distribution of roles.

Thinking of all these things, I concluded that if I had married Yoohyeh, the same thing would happen to me, if not worse than with Doménico. I should have worked to pay his bills, so pressure in decision and harder and: call King Yoohyeh.

"Hello Beautiful, how are you love?"

"I called you to tell you, with the pain of my soul, that our story is over and that I will stay with Doménico."

"Wait ! don't move from there, I'm coming right now."

"No, don't come!"

"You have to tell me by looking me in the eye."

I was in my pajamas and quickly changed to wait for him. As soon as he knocked, I opened the door and did not let him in, as much as I wanted it. I closed the door behind me and we went out into the street. I knew if we were alone, I wouldn't have the strength to push him back- if he took me in his arms.

"You're going to make a mistake, Bella, please..."

"That's my Yoohyeh decision, I'm so sorry."

I didn't want to hear it anymore; the feelings that throbbed inside me were immense. The only relative next to me, Caridad, had left and now you leave the man I love or so much.

I called a taxi and corsi via, as if not to give me a chance to repent; I turned only to look for the last time at my great love; I greet it to and lofissai for a long time, as if I wanted to stop the image and never erase it from memory.

"I have to take care of my career, the one that Doménico helped me achieve. At the end of the day, I owe him everything."

Domenico, on the other hand, was like a father, a brother, a mother: all in the end.

I wiped away my tears and went to doménico's offices.

In October 1963 we went to Istanbul to shoot the film *F.B.I. Call Istanbul.* The producers were Turkish and because they had not yet distributed Ali Baba's film in their theaters, they had a party in my honor. Leo took from Rome, on Domenico's behalf, a few thousand photos, signed by me by distributing the kings during the first of the film.

It was an extraordinary event. Those present took the photos from Leo's hands, so much so that he scratched his hands and for this reason decided to throw them into the air in a way. Doménico liked what was going on; he looked amused as they pushed each other to grab the photos.

After the screening, I took the stage and spoke thanking everyone for being vehement that night to see me and after loud applause -he threw kisses at the audience and for this, they gathered around me, pushing each other trying to get closer. The theatre director came up from the back of the stage and caught my eye with a whistle and beckoned me to get to where he was. He took me off a staircase leading to a private elevator to the producer's house where Doménico and Leo were waiting for me.

I was very impressed by the city of Istanbul, by the new buildings mixed with the ancient ones in harmony. The flies and with their high domes seemed to reach the sky. Muslims frequented them twice a day to praise Allah. Hagia Sophia was the largest and most beautiful I had ever seen. Businesses, especially jewelry stores, had their doors open all the time and without any problem of theft because in the Muslim religion they do not forgive that lack. To the one who steals they cut off his hands. In the company of Leo, who accompanied me everywhere, we went to the bazaar to buy souvenirs to take them to Rome.

So, we crossed the bridge between Istanbul and Ankara, turkey's other major city, which is bordered by the Golden Horn, an arm of the sea that bathes the two coasts.

On one of the times, we went to the bazaar, Leo introduced me to Peter Ustinov, who was in Istanbul and was shooting with Melina Mercury, the movie *Top Kapi*. The company spent three months in Turkey, everything was very nice, but I couldn't forget Yoohyeh.

End Of Relationship
With Domenico

On my return to Rome, I realized that Domenico had nothing to give me the money for the films he had made, not even the last one, but he had also disappeared without saying anything. Scoprii from the newspapers that he had a trial and that there were 28 lawyers, one for each creditor. The fake cheques he had signed amounted to four hundred million lire and my name appeared in the newspapers asifamica and his wife.

The outrage and anger against Doménico were evident, now that I have made a name for myself in the cinema, I appeared in the newspapers with such a scandal.

"I can't take it anymore; I've come to this point for Doménico."

Without thinking too much about it, I looked for an apartment in I Parioli that I liked because some friends lived there and I ed iialone in Viale Bruno *Buozzi,* where Roberto Rossellini, ex-husband of Ingrid Berman, lived.

Doménico had five years from the judge to pay, but throughout that time he could not make films as a producer. He had heard from Leo where he lived and introduced himself to me with a bouquet of flowers and some magazines and gifts. But I got it very coldly,

"Doménico, our relationship is already over and there is no return..."

- We're not going to be enemies for this, if I propose a movie to you, do you make it?

I looked at him and answered bitterly "if you'll pay me, of course."

Then I walked him to the door and looked at him, as he came down, to see if he looked back and when he didn't, I felt sorry for him.

Bella Knows Her First Husband

In April 1964 the film Appuntamento a *Dallas was* made, with Claudio Gora. Nico Fidenco was entrusted with the musical column for the film, in which he would have to sing. That's why they needed me to do a singing rehearsal, and that's how they introduced me to Robert F. Poitevin, who had an amazing musical experience.

Poitevin had started in 1947, in Paris, as a pianist for EdithPiaf, with whom they toured the United States also playing at the Waldoof Astoria.

Later he had been a pianist for Henry Salvador and Belafonte, playing at the Lido in Paris with Dessy Guillespi and in the Django Reinard orchestra, then created his own complex: The Robbys playing in Rome, the Grotta dei Piccione and the Brigadoon.

He then went to Saudi Arabia for 5 years, between 1952 and 1957, and signed a contract in Kuwait. While he was there, he got lost in the desert. He spent two nights and three days drinking water from the radiator, thus surviving. He was attacked by an eagle and defended himself with his gun, killing her.

Some passing Bedouins saved him and as a gift Robert offered them the dead eagle.

On his return to Baghdad, he bought shares in Coca-Cola but there was a change of government and he lost everything.

He had to return to Rome because, when he was three years old, he fell ill and when he took him to the hospital he died in his arms and to conclude, his wife filed for divorce.

He left the *Orchestra I Robby* and began working at R.C.A. Italian as a musical assistant, among others Paul Anka, Frank Sinatra and Henry Mancini.

During the tests Robert did to me, we looked at each other frequently; here Cupid had started throwing his darts.

I looked at him as if to ask him for help, because I had never sung and he looked at me to give me musical time. In the end the test was useless because I did not know a complete song, but great was my emotion in learning about the studies of the R.C.A.

From that day we exchanged phone numbers and started seeing each other. The sweet talk with the accent French and those blue eyes of Robert, made me forget the latest adventures with Doménico and Yoohyeh. They spent two months and one day I invited him to stay with me and that night he moved into the Eor apartment.

That night scoprii to have problems in that sexual relationship; don't potevor forget Yoohyeh, but don't know it to Robert so as not to hurt him and Avevor even other concerns. I didn't work or more like before and Robert's salary wasn't very good, one hundred and fifty thousand lire a month is not enough to live on. To complete, in those days, I received a letter from the authorities informing me that I had to either ask permission to work or marry me if you want to or staying Italy.

All those thoughts shunted me and didn't leave me alone, and I didn't even go back to relaxing me to make love to Robert who said to me:

"Don't worry, I'm going to work at the movies creating music columns and you don't have to work."

There were good intentions in his words, but it was a long-term hope; I know that Robert took time to earn only to keep the house.

Five months after my separation from Domenico, he calls me and makes me a proposal.

"I offer you the leading role in the film *Sinbad against the seven Saracens,* with Gordon Mitchell and under my direction."

"What can I tell you Doménico...? I have to work."

That day was bad luck for me, signing the contract that would cause me a lot of disappointment, betrayal, pain. If I had known, I would never have signed it.

They had started making the film and because I didn't have to make an agent, I had to deal, as far as the contract and my salary with the producer was concerned, a very cunning and cold guy who was a friend of Domenico's and knew how to make money, without losing a penny.

"Bella, I'm offering you two million lire, that's more than you get from Doménico."

"No thanks."

I got up and looked at him badly.

"Well, I'm going to give you half a million, this is safe money, remember that with Salvi you didn't get anything."

I wanted to explode when in front of that sarcastic man and I wanted to insult him and even hurt him and I thought "So cynical, I just met him and he's aware of everything that happened."

So, I said, "All right, I do, I sign because Salvi asked me, but I want him to know that I don't work for him and that I'm getting two million less than I normally get."

During the filming of this film a lot of accidents happened and this made me think of Doménico or the crew members, people, with whom I had worked for many years and who treated me coldly. One day I was sitting outside the locker room trailer when one of the knights threw a mud ball in my face. They had to wait at least two hours, while they cleaned my face and put on makeup again. I didn't get back on set until they found out who it was.

A few days after filming a scene in which I fled with Sinbad on horseback crossing the battlefield, one of the guards hit me in the arm with the edge of the shield, leaving me with a bruise.

Once again, I protested to Doménico "Check the people you hire or I will make the decision to report them to the authorities or I will stop working with you."

"I'm so sorry, and I assure you that the manager who hurt you won't be working for the rest of the movie anymore."

Doménico sent to call the head of the extras who apologized.

During the filming of a scene in the theater, with the actor playing Sinbad, another incident happened. It was about taking the weapons to a cave where land Avevor hidden. The weapons were bows and arrows and a huge sabre in his holth, which was tied with a thin thread painted black so that it could not be seen.

The scene was repeated fourteen times and - in the last time- the thread broke as the actor dropped his weapons. The sabre sped like a bullet, hit me in the face and caused a wound to my forehead near my right eyebrow, cut off half of my left eyebrow and caused bruises to my nose.

I put my hands on my face and uttered a cry of pain, went forward and stumbled upon a production chair because I couldn't see. My face was covered in blood that also flowed on my hands. Those on the crew didn't know what to do; they took me by the arm to make me sit with my head back, while some looked for ice; another went to call Doménico.

A few minutes later Domenico arrived and, seeing me in that situation, exclaimed:

"Was the actress in my movie ruined?"

Forgetting everything around him, he took me in the car to the hospital, because it seemed to him that the ambulance was late. As he was taking me to an emergency, he stroked me and called me Bibi, as he did before.

I stayed fifteen days in the hospital after plastic surgery on my forehead. I got flowers from the actor who had come to apologize. I forgave him because I knew it was his first film and there were others to blame. From the same or hospital, I called my lawyer.

"All right, I'm going to sue the producer."

I went back to the set to finish the movie and one day, while in my dressing room, watching out the window, I saw the Doménico hugging a girl as she entered the studio.

"He's consoled himself, and now it's going to be hard for me to work with him."

So, I made the decision to marry Robert that he sent to call his mother who lived in France and so I began to learn French.

The French don't need papers to be in Italy because of the agreements between the countries, but I had to get married to stay. One morning call my friend Liliana.

"Liliana, I'm marrying Robert."

After a silence, as if Liliana had gasped.

"Careful, Robert's a 17-year-old man older than you. Robert is not meat or fish for you."

I didn't pay attention to what my friend had told me, because I knew what I was doing, so I went to Count Anselmetti's house to pass on the invitation.

He was a small man of stature, with black and smooth hair, he came from a very rich family in the province of

Turin, who did not accept that he was effeminate and to save the reputation of the family offered him the opportunity, in the will, that if he married a woman, they would give him a part of the inheritance.

Man, I brought you the invitation to my wedding.

The Count without opening it said "I have a proposal for you. Why don't you marry me and we go to Turin in my birthplace to take the other part of my inheritance which is a ring of brilliants worth two hundred thousand dollars."

We split up and do your sex life with whoever you want because you know what my preferences are.

"That's not what I'm looking for, but thank you anyway."

"I have someone who wants to meet you is a very nice engineer."

"Another day, now I'm in a hurry."

On October 11, 1964, at 11:00 a.m., we married Robert. The ceremony was held at the Capitol. A few minutes before marrying me, walk along the red carpet until the Mayor of Rome, smiling, was waiting for me in a black dress and the colors of Italy around the waist.

The table was polished with enamel and had two bronze candlesticks on each side, the chairs had a high backrest, and they were antique and gold in color.

At times I would have liked to scream and run away and what would the guests have said? And to console mi pensto:

Well, if I don't do well, divorce because the marriage isn't Catholic and it's going to be transferred to the French embassy, so what am I worried about?

At Brigadoon Restaurant there was the reception and among the guests the actors including GordonMitchell. Nico Fidenco, introduced me to a fashionable singer named Sergio Endrigo and his wife. Then there was Nora Orlandi, who had a choir and was married to a nephew of the Buitoni family;

her friend Liliana Molteni and her husband Ambrogio, who was a writer for my films, Count Anselmetti and many others.

After the partimmo reception for Paris, on a honeymoon, where we met the rest of Robert's family. Robert's family, they were very kind to me.

On his return to Rome, Robert changed the car and the house because the new one was located on the Via Renato Fucini più vicinaalla R.C.A., although it was far from my casaai Parioli.

From that moment the money began to be spent and when it was finished, to help Robert in the expenses, he paid for the jewelry that Doménico had given me and that I also liked so much. Stavor destroying my future, everything I had created with Doménico, I am now losing it.

I felt depressed yet I still struggled and reflected optimistically.

He's my husband and I have to help him, he tells me he's going to make money with the movies soon.

The youth, the lack of experience and the lack of good advice made sure that I didn't see that I was ruining my career which had started so well (eleven starring films).

Now I didn't make any more movies, and when he called me, I answered.

"I don't care; I live with my husband now- no thanks."

I didn't realize that what he got was lost, because Robert never had any money. That man more mature than me and who was now thirty-eight years old, what he wanted was to climb positions in the world of bohemian cinema, using me to do it. From there we moved into a house- four blocks from where we lived.

A year and three months had passed and I felt more alone than ever before and, even though I had met new friends, I felt that it was not enough for me. I thought,

"We are both alone in Italy; it's time to start a family."

And so, after two years and a month of marriage, in the hospital of Frascati, in the province of Rome, Jean Paul Poitevin was born that it was November 25, 1966.

Robert left R.C.A. and worked as an independent, composer and musical arranger for films.

Then turn to Frascati, a small town located between lakes and mountains, twenty-six kilometers from Rome where most of the land is rich in vine yards and greenery.

In Mussolini's time, the house where we lived was occupied by the Germans. From the balcony of the second floor, you could see the beauty of Rome with its seven hills, the Roman aqueduct or, the ancient ruins, in short, the entire city.

Because of the change of city, the doctor who treated me during my pregnancy could not come there. The doctor knew that he could not or has the baby normally because of the ovarian operation and had recommended that, at nine months, he and axes in the hospital to make a caesarean section. On expiration date

I did what the doctor had recommended to me but drove in Frascati concluded:

"Go home, when the pain begins, come."

One morning I felt bad, but it wasn't the pains of labor. I had dizziness and discomfort in my body that didn't explain what it was. You start going down the stairs and the vertigo was bigger. I grab my to the railing so as not to fall, put my hand in my lap; something was wrong with the creature, until I got off and called the Roberts to take me to the hospital.

I arrived at the hospital and the doctor examined me, and he frightened me, telling me that he did not guarantee my life or that of the unborn child. When you hear this, I was shocked and uncontrollable tremors began, so the doctor ordered me to prepare and operator gently.

When I was in the preparation room, I looked up at the wall and saw a picture of our Lord Jesus Christ and or, as I had never done before, I pressed him with great faith, not to take my son away from me, and promised to educate him in the Christian religion. He wept silently and for a few minutes the pain subsided, they arrived to take me to the operating room and I began to tremble again.

One doctor asked the other "Why tremble so much?"

"Don't worry, some people are very sensitive."

At the time of removal, the child had ingested liquid that he had in his lungs. The anesthesiologist put a thin tube through his nose into his lungs, thus removing the liquid that did not allow him to breathe; they immediately made him breathe artificially and the baby began to show signs of life, so the doctor grabbed him by the feet, gave him two spanking and the baby began to cry.

It was a miracle of God, the baby weighed 2,750 kilograms, his little body was long and his face very cute and well formed, it looked like an ivory cameo, it was just like me.

Dr. Luigi, an anesthesiologist, wanted the child to have his name and was angry that Robert, at the time of recording, called him Jean-Paul.

The baby was put in an incubator for five days and when we left the hospital, he was handsome and smiling, full of life but it wasn't enough for his mother. I looked for the best pediatrician in Rome to take care of him.

The pediatrician's last name was Zam and I never knew what his nationality was. What he knew was that the doctor would be in Geneva for pediatric medical conferences and everyone was following his theories. In less than a month he put Jean - Paul in his ideal weight with a formula of milk and vitamins that suited him very well.

Once he recovered, after treatment, I baptized the child in Frascati Cathedral, thus keeping the promise that Avevor made before his birth.

Her godmother was Nora Orlandi, a singer and songwriter to whom Robert had made arrangements for the films, including one with Clint Eastwood.

The godfather was Pino Roccon, a lawyer-pianist, Robert's friend, dedicated to music rather than his profession. Among the guests of the baptism were Susanna and Franco Nicalizzi, music director of la Paramaunt in Rome and composer of the film *Trinità*.

Nora began composing more music for the films and called on Robert to make arrangements for the orchestra. Things are going a little better financially.

Robert often had to go to Rome for recordings of his music and therefore decided to take a house on the Via Renato Fucini, where we lived in Rome earlier, but further north.

The apartment consisted of three bedrooms and two bathrooms at the top and at the bottom had a living room, dining room, kitchen and a study that connected to a terrace that covered the entire length of the apartment. There were no lack of job offers for Robert, since he made the first film with Nora Orlandi, so he began to spend; he bought furniture for the living room and changed the car. Robert was never satisfied. The baby was already one year old and walking all over the house and so time was not enough for me to do so many things in the house. Thinking about it, we decided to take Lydia, a service girl who lives with us, even so she could go out in the evening.

We soon went to Paris to attend the wedding of Michelle, Robert's niece, and took Lydia to take care of Jean-Paul.

The ceremony was beautiful, the bride looked like an angel, she was blonde with blue eyes like two drops of sea water and the groom, and she was good-looking, with black and smooth hair and a smile that showed off her white and uniform teeth.

Back in Rome, Lydia was supposed to be responsible for the suitcases, because it looked like she didn't want to do anything else but lost a suitcase on the train. At home, he also did not want to take care of the child when we had to go out and, finally, left the child in a high chair to feed him but fell, getting hurt.

We took him to Dr. Zam, but it was nothing serious, but when we returned, we fired Lydia.

Robert was not satisfied with the apartment and asked to move into the next building on the top floor, with the terrace on the main street. Of course, it cost him more but he didn't care.

After changing, he called a decorator to decorate the living room and dining room. He did his job by putting the colors from the pale blue of the carpet to the white of the furniture, the curtains were orange in color, but what stood out most was a handmade mural that occupied the entire wall of the room and represented a tropical panorama with a beach where the sun set reflecting in the water an orange color among the palm trees that lulled into the wind.

I thought with all these innovations Robert would stay calm, at least for a while, but he wasn't. When the economic accounts of the films arrived, he wanted to spend more on vanities, without facing major debts, such as that of the Hospital of Frascati, which had sent him invoices that he did not pay.

He then thought about going to the French Riviera to spend a holiday or buy a new car and this is how he met a man named Vescovi to whom he sold his car and bought him a white Fulvia della Lancia making monthly payments.

He owed money to the decorator and for the living room and dining room furniture. With the premise that he didn't like the modern, he replaced them with the old ones that were mine.

One day a friend of Robert's named Roberto Mannoni came home, with whom he had met before meeting me and who was destined to be his brother-in-law, but the girl's mother knew that he could not marry because of the church and said goodbye by putting him on the street, being Robert's mother very religious.

Roberto was tall, with black hair, white teeth and was also very kind. Fu invited several times to lunch on several occasions, until one day he noticed that there was an empty room and asked Robert to allow him to be there for a few days and my husband, who did not know how to say no, agreed without consulting me. In this way Robert came to live at home.

Everything went well until I was without the service girl, who had gone crazy. He kept the cooked food in drawers instead of the refrigerator, and when I caught his attention, he took it badly, locked himself in the room and didn't want to leave. I was afraid of that woman and I called Leo to help me. With Leo's calmness and a pull herbal tea I prepared, we managed to take her out and then home with her suitcases packed so she wouldn't come back.

As Roberto saw that I was alone, he wanted to help me in everything, even in the kitchen and with the baby, but everything had a double game, he wanted to earn my trust because he had become invading me. One night the child was in bed and Robert in the studio wrote music. Roberto and I were sitting on the couch in the living room watching television. Roberto got up, went to the bar, prepared two drinks and offered one to me.

I didn't want to, but since you made it, thank you.

I kept watching television noticing that Roberto was sitting closer to me; he put his hands on my neck and began to caress my long hair.

"I want to own you; I can't take it anymore, now that we're alone."

He tried to approach to kiss me and then I stood up.

"I can't believe, my husband's friend, whom we gave refuge to..."

I checked myself not to slap him on the face covered with a well-groomed beard.

"You have to respect me because you're in my house and I can throw you out like a dog.

That said I went to my room. That night Robert came to bed very tired and it was late, so I don't tell him anything."

The next morning, all three of us were sitting on the terrace having breakfast. Avevor already talked to Robert in the room about what had happened between me and Roberto the night before, but to my surprise, Robert did not believe me, he took it as a joke and asked him.

"Is it true what Bella says?"

"How can you think that? It was just a joke on my part." he answered cynically.

The discussion became animist; I get up from my chair.

"You'd rather believe Roberto than me that I'm your wife."

I went to my room and called the Leos:

I want you to come to dinner tonight; I need to talk to you.

Leo agreed and came soon. Avevor desires to die.

"I can't believe Leo, my husband, doesn't believe in me and now that man will continue to live here and I can't do anything..."

In the next room, the child wanted something he couldn't reach and started screaming, Robert was also in the room and instead of finding out what he wanted, he threw a book at him as Leo and I walked in: The book ended up at the boy's feet without touching him, but we noticed it would be dangerous if he pulled it higher.

When we were alone, Leo spoke to me.

"Beware that Robert doesn't remove that beautiful smile that Jean-Paul has, because it would be a shame if he mistreated him."

"I assure you I'll never let him."

Soon we got a Swedish babysitter so we could date Robert at night and not be alone with Roberto.

The moment came when Robert had to go to Milan and so we left the baby with the nanny and Roberto. Already in the hotel he calls the people at home to find out how things were and Roberto replied saying that the babysitter had left. On her return call the agency to find out why the babysitter had left and the response was shocking.

"Mr. Roberto has submitted dishonest proposals to our employee."

Then I really couldn't take it anymore, I called Roberto and threw him out of the house.

"I can't keep you here anymore Roberto; you're leaving, right now!"

Calm was backing home. After this incident I received a letter from the lawyer Pace, incaricato demy affairs at the Court of Rome, for my participation in the film Vulcano Figlio *di Giove,* of September 1962. The lawyer then summoned me to give me my money.

I got the check and my first thought was to invest it in something useful, like a house. With the recommendation of our friend Susana Micalizzi, we bought on anzio beach, the top floor of a building under construction, ordering the two apartments that made up the floor to be joined to make one, with the keys to the elevator directed to our floor.

In the end we had a property and the eror very happy. I bought plants to put them on the balconies, furniture and bamboo bar, which gave the apartment a summery vibe.

Despite everything, Robert had never been satisfied and the desire to change was always present in him. And so much so that he convinced me to sell the apartment on the beach to buy a caravan with seven seats to sleep and put it on another beach called Lido del Pini, where Susana and her husband had parked their trailer.

With the remaining money, Robert bought an Alfa Romeo sedan, without paying for the previous car.

Since Robert did not have a permanent job, but instead composed and arranged music and conducted the orchestra for album and film work, he received a large sum every six months from SIAE, (Società Italiana Autori e Editori) for this reason we could spend the whole summer in the trailer and visit the house in Rome on weekends.

In the summer, Robert's entire family came to spend the summer with them, brought their camping luggage and put it near the trailer: the family was not complete; only Laurence, the mother, arrived; Simone, the sister with her husband Jean and their two daughters Annie and Michelle.

&&&

I go back there now and talk about then, as if the past were present and I looked at my life as if in a mirror, a movie...

Jean-Paul is two years old, he likes the beach and he has a lot of space to play, I am adapting to the outdoors, the only one who is bored is Robert because he has to make musical arrangements for composers such as Nino Rotta, Maurice Jarre, Nino Olivieri, Ennio Moriconi, Bruno Canfora, Ramón Legrand and Nora Orlandi.

Things are now good for him, as he promised me before marrying me, but there are dissatisfaction and greed in him. She wants to have more than she can spend and doesn't realize that volevor be calm, take care of the house, and the baby. But he's blind and he doesn't realize he's missing me.

And the past still returns...

And then we moved again, in Via Renato Fucini, to where we lived or before the wedding to I Parioli,

Robert won't change anymore, he still has to pay for the Lancia machine and the decorator looking for it and it's useless.

"I'm fighting the current." I confided in Leo.

One night the baby was crying because he was not feeling well, after getting up two or three times he took him to sleep with us, but he continued to cry; Robert raised his hand and hit him on the nose, causing him to bleed and in an instant the pillow was covered in blood.

I took him to the bathroom, cleaned him and saw that it wasn't that bad, but his nerves were disturbed and made him anxious. When we got better, we had a strong discussion.

I remembered the words that my friend Liliana Monteni had told me, that if I got married, I would take the pentita and it was true, now I gave her reason. Remember or even whenever on Capitol Hill, when I walked or on the red carpet, and thought I'd get out of there.

Why did I do that? I had left my dreams, the world of cinema, in Rome, with the merits and defects that was nevertheless my world, the one that had given me moments of happiness and well-being. I may have had to abandon it under Italian law but a road, I know, I would have found it to stay in a country I loved. And I also regretted those, now old movies, that I was queen of and now...

In America

My family had moved all over Cuba to New Jersey, Caridad and her husband Felix; Juan, his wife Irma and their two daughters Iliana and Zuni.

When Christmas arrived, in addition to gifts to the baby, Robert brought me three tickets to go to New York, with the premise that he wanted to meet my family. After all, it's been ten years since I saw my brother Juan.

Preparations were made for the trip, the gifts we would bring, and- after a month we were on the plane - where some drunken passengers mocked us for not speaking More English.

The family welcomed us warmly. Caridad with her husband lived in a third-floor apartment and Juan with his wife and daughters, in the building next door, also on the third floor and they talked through the window.

When we arrived, the roads were dirty with snow melted by cars and heating, the cleaning staff and garbage collectors were on strike so that the bad smells of the accumulated waste spread through the air. I didn't like New York and New Jersey for these things.

It was pleasant, however, to be together in the family, to remember the past times and among those memories was also mine when Charity was in Italy. And it was nice to remember, the time of cinema and all the beautiful things that had happened. One of those days Felix had a few drinks and in his drunkenness he said with Caridad; then it turns out he was jealous of Robert.

It seems Felix was jealous of his wife for no reason and with all the men approaching, especially when he drank. You knew him well for living with them for more than seven years in Havana.

After this incident we moved into Juan's apartment waiting for the month of vacation to pass. Juan and his wife did not have much, but they shared without hypocrisy and goodwill.

The money ran out before the return date and talking to Caridad, the idea came out of her that Robert wanted to hear "Why don't you stay?"

That's what Robert expected, the opportunity to stay, because that was his intention when he thought he was coming to the United States. The next day he took his passport and took it to a lawyer to do the paperwork for the residence and called the SIAE to send the copyrights to New Jersey, then handed me the passport saying:

"Go to Italy and sell everything we have there and bring the money, I'm trying to get the documents, meanwhile I'm looking for a job."

I was undecided...

"Restart everything in a country where I don't know anything or the customs and language that I don't speak well. Why does Robert want to stay, having everything in Italy?"

It didn't give me time to think. Caridad then added:

"I take care of the baby until you get back."

Robert concluded:

"I assure you it's going to be okay, don't worry."

On the other hand, Juan expressed the desire to live together and they insisted so much that I gave in and went to

Italy to lose the last thing I had left as a memory of cinema and Doménico." that happy stage of my life that would never come back. On the plane, I'd go thinking about my three-year-old son, who I wouldn't see until I got back.

I arrived in Rome, in contact with my friends and published an ad in the newspaper to sell everything. Many people came, including Dr. Saladin who bought various valuable things.

"Doesn't it hurt to detach yourself from these objects that have unforgettable memories for you?"

"Yes, but what can I do, my son and my husband are in America and I have to be with them; besides I won't be alone in, my brothers are there."

I felt a deep sorrow in my soul, having to free my house knowing that I did not have one or in the United States, but what hurt me the most was the sale of those furniture that I kept to or on my husband's whim to stay in America, but I had to sell them and quickly because I was worried about the child, since he was not er or ever been separated from him for so long.

At night I called Susana who came with her husband and they said,

"Don't be silly, why don't you stay?"

The solitude was great and the sadness invaded and wept until I fell asleep. The next day I called my friend Leo to ask him for Yoohyeh's address.

"I want to see him, I don't know why all these years without seeing him, my feelings haven't changed and I want to know if it's the same for him."

"Yoohyeh's in Persia filming a movie."

"Then I'll leave you my address in the United States so you can give it to him when I get back."

"It's very nice," Leo said.

The antique furniture, along with the Louis XVI sofa, was purchased by Dr. Saladin; Susana bought the dining room with showcase, wall-to-wall, a blue carpet, and a glass vase that had inside a tree made of shells and snails of all colors and coral branches, all gathered on a marble base.

That and other items I put them in a bamboo trunk and sent them with a ship to America.

The days passed and I had not been able to sell the Alfa Romeo and the trailer. I had sad thoughts like, as if something were to happen to the child if it were not, it or not to immediately. I called a friend of the cinema, Spartaco Antonuci, who together with his friend had kept the trailer and the car, promising me that he would send me compensation every month until he paid everything.

They introduced me to a Mexican journalist named Gloria who had kept the living room furniture, giving some of the value and promising the same. When I decided to review the accounts, I had the knowledge that he had sold everything for a third of real value, not to mention Spartacus and Gloria.

The apartment was already empty and I went to hand over the keys when Bishops arrived, to whom Robert owed the Lancia machine:

I need you to give me my money.

"Robert will come back soon and give you your money, wait a little longer."

"It's to Robert that my lawyer intends to take action against him."

He slammed the car door, and cleared the wheels and left.

Upon arrival in the United States, I realized that what I had fore towered had happened; the child had a very high fever, for no apparent reason, because he was not ill. To lower it to, they had given him medicine to no availing, so Caridad put on the forehead of the ice to lower the temperature and then clutched it with alcohol. When he saw me, he hugged me, kissed and did not want to leave me, as if he wanted to tell me: "None go more away."

A few days after they were with them, Irma discovered that four blocks away there was an empty apartment and told them:

"Why don't you take it tight?"

"Robert, shall we see him?"

I was sorry because for a long time I had to live with them, drink and eat without contributing anything. My brother had undergone surgery and had to pay $400, and in the Esquina warehouse, thankfully the owner was his friend and didn't harass him for payment. Robert was aware of this situation but did not even attempt to help him.

The apartment was all in one, kitchen, dining room and living room; the only thing he had separated was the bedroom. We moved in carrying the used furniture that Irma's friends gave us. It was all in disarray when I got a letter from my friend Susana, telling me she was going on vacation and had planned to visit them.

I wanted to die of shame:

Susana, who is so aristocratic and envious, will come and see me in this ugly apartment with old furniture... Susana, as soon as she arrives in Italy, will tell all my friends. Because of Robert... all this...

A few days before Susana and Franco arrived, Robert borrowed Juan's car to go to New York looking for work and found it at the Sherry Netherland Hotel, located on 5th Avenue, almost across from the Dupon Plaza Hotel, to play the piano from 5:00 p.m. until 1:00 p.m. That day I was content with the news, but I didn't lend him much attention, error bitter, taciturn and I thought:

"As we were in Rome and look now..."

When Susana called to say she was in New York, I was hoping that they wouldn't come so soon, but what to do, that was the reality and I had to accept it.

During the two weeks they were in New York, they visited us twice and Susana didn't stop criticizing me without worrying about whether Robert or I was angry. That day Stavor availing the bed and one of the sheets was torn; Susana saw him and said, "Are these flowers of America?"

"Better times will come, you know what Robert is like, we're here today and tomorrow we don't know where."

On the day Susana came to greet each other, Jean-Paul ran after some children playing.

"American mothers let their children play on sidewalks and in the streets, I wouldn't live in the United States even if they gave me a villa."

"I didn't answer him and when they finally left, I sighed and looked up at the sky. Wow what a relief!"

A week later came a letter from the customs of the port of N.Y. informing me of the arrival of the packages he had sent, by ship, from Rome. I was very happy because some of the things I didn't want to get rid of came off. Juan gave me the car and drove me.

We opened the trunks and what a disappointment, two glasses of Napoleon were broken, but it did not give him the importance because there were four left and even my favorite book was intact; it was a book of Canti Gregoriani, lined in leather, recommended and signed by Pope Eugene IV, born in Venice (1431-1447).

Two paintings also arrived that I had bought in Istanbul and two paintings that Doménico's brother had given me telling me that they were from the 1800s. And there were so many little things that brought me so many fond memories.

The rent amount for the apartment was relatively low, which allowed Robert to give the deposit for a car; an Oldsmobil Ninety-nine decapot table in white, who wanted to paint yellow and when they handed it the color was almost orange and so it remained because it needed it.

As Robert wrote to SIAE, to receive royalties' money, he got his first check and said, "We don't think anymore, let's get out of this apartment."

We found it on two floors, with three bedrooms, bathroom, kitchen and dining room. Nothing was missing; it was new, clean and well located. I liked it because one of the stairs went down Bergenline Avenue, which was N.J.'s main street.

Once again, we lived as before, in a decent house. We just had to buy the furniture, and we did it by furnishing every room.

Now I just needed to buy a stereo and a TV to furnish the whole room.

Robert spent time watching horror movies with the kid, who was only four years old and who I didn't like.

One evening, around 7:00, I was crouching in front of the tub mixing cold and hot water to bathe the baby but Jean Paul had press or a knife, he approached me from behind, very slowly walking on the carpet and when he raised his armed hand, the shadow of the child made me turn and terrified shouts to "Noooooo!"

Jean-Paul gasped at the scream and immediately dropped the knife. He grabbed him and gave him a good spanking as I scolded him,

"Don't you play with the knife, you understand me? I'm your mother, never do it again, never again."

Robert arrived at dawn and I took the opportunity to say "Tomorrow we will put Jean-Paul in kindergarten so that he can get used to playing with children his age and not watch horror movies. I always told you not to show them to him, and today I found out that his mind is being plagiarized."

So, I told him what had happened in the bathroom with the baby. Robert shrugged his shoulders and replied:

"Those are childish things; no one's eating his mind."

And he turned to sleep saying goodnight. I stared at my husband's back, incredulous at his reaction and at the same time felt that my heart was beating hard in my chest. You press my lips not to say what I thought and light up. The next day we went to visit some schools to enroll Jean Paul and found a kindergarten that I liked. The child stayed to play with the other children. Here's what I wanted for my son: young children his age, not horror movies!

However, I began to realize that nothing would change Robert; he had yet to pay the decorator who was looking for him, the Lbencia to Bishops and it was all useless. I was fighting against the current, and I said to Leo my good friend:

"I feel more alone than ever and the only consolation is my son, who I love so much."

Watching the days go by, I got bored or at home and decided to enroll in the D'cossimo school that was on Bergenline Avenue,to attend an English and typing course. Ona day at school, the principal said to me: "What are you going to do when you finish classes? Are you going to look for a job?"

"I don't know why my English isn't that good!"

So, the principal advised me to take the IBM keypunch which didn't need so much English and showed me the machines I really liked. So, I finished that class by taking my diploma.

After I finished my studies, I decided to look for a job on Wall Street in New York. With the school recommendation, it was easy for me and I started working leaving the child in the care of my husband and kindergarten. On one of those days when he wasn't working, Robert and The Boy went to the park in Calle 80, where there was a lake that, due to the cold, had a layer of ice on the surface. The park was separated from the lake by a low concrete wall from where, during the summer, the children, sitting on it, fed the ducks. Quail day, due to the cold, the park was almost empty and Jean Paul wanted Robert to make him sit on the wall in front of the water, and Robert lor did sit on a park bench not far from the baby.

The wall was slippery for ice and Jean Paul fell into the freezing water, as a result, I got a phone call of what had happened. I immediately axed the work. The baby had been taken to my sister's house where they gave him a hot water bath and a camphor-spirited massage and put him to bed giving him a cup of chocolate as well. Jean Paul fell asleep as if nothing had happened.

When he gets to the scarecrow, I think about what might have happened.

It was an alarm, but that was enough for me to leave my job permanently and dedicate myself to my son. The days slowly passed for me that stavor accepting my situation as a mother and resigned that of wife, when one day I received a letter from Yoohyeh. Look at the envelope where Richard Lloyd was written to the sender and don't understand who he could be, until you open the letter in front of Robert who was also curious. When I saw Yoohyeh's signature, I was so nervous that I was shaking my husband:

"Scusami, but I have to go to the bathroom."

Leave the room to the by entering the bathroom and closing the door behind me you begin to read. Yoohyeh wrote to me that, after their separation, he had felt very sad and had gone to his country where he had worked as an actor and director and for those reasons, he did not see him in Rome. He saw Leo Coliman and had talked a lot about her, telling him that he still remembered her with great love and non l'avev to never forgotten and had also told him that in a film he was shooting there was a scene in which a car had to catch fire and the driver could not open the car door, jump and stava burning alive. Then realizing that no one would save him with a blanket on his head had gone to the aid of the wretch, causing third-degree burns all over his body spending three months in the tehran hospital.

His mother had told him that when he was delirious about the fever, the only name he made was his. Among other things, he had told Leo that he did not want to lose contact with her and that he wrote to his mother's house and gave him the address: Richard Lloyd Ave, Lalezar now 105 Tabagheh Sevon Tehran Iran.

He had, by the way, bought a few hectares of land in the Caspian Sea to build the house of his dreams.

When my husband knocked on the bathroom door and opened it without waiting for an answer, he found me with the letter in his hand, very sarcastic mii said: - You hide in the bathroom to read the letters, e!? -

He put the letter to him to read, which he did not do and closed the door. Expected on the following day to answer Richard. That name didn't seem to belong to Yoohyeh, I had always called him differently. But yes, that's what I wanted, I'd call him.

We started a thick match. I invited him to come but he replied that he had business that he could not give *up*, *that* he had left the cinema and was importing Carrara marble for Persia and that therefore it was not yet the time. Meanwhile, Robert was tired of playing the piano at the Sherry Netherlands Hotel, where he had met Danny Kaye's son and George Gershwin.

Meanwhile, Christmas came slowly and so I made a stuffed turkey and bought some liquor to celebrate. Robert rented an accordion so we danced through the most joyful night.

I had a portable washing machine as a gift, which caused Robert to come back from Machines Furniture and open an account with Machin, the owner of that business, to pay weekly. In one of those times the owner told him that he had an apartment at the top of his house that was empty, that he would rent it to Robert who always invented reasons to move. I was beginning to think that I really didn't know what to do to the man, who had the change craze.

I thought, "Of course Jean Paul is still small and it doesn't really matter if he moves so often but when he starts school, he would have to stay in one place or there will be more serious problems. And so, I decided for the only son I had. It was a miracle of God that he had been saved at birth; and I never forgot my promise to educate him in the Christian religion, so he chose a Catholic school. Since Robert gave him everything he wanted, I was the one who disciplined the boy who, for his part, made a habit of running to his father to be defended when I scolded him, and for these reasons I made myself strong and told myself. He's still small for a school, but it's for his own good."

And it was also necessary because she alone could not cope with the bad education that Robert was giving to the child or therefore decided to enroll him even though she was only five years old at that Catholic school, in St. Vincent de

Paul, New York, where they could teach him to obey and have respect.

We would visit him every weekend and take him home and when it was time to drop him off again at school and happy but I was the one who was suffering. Per give me strength, I though tor the things he did when he was at home, like when he was at Caridad's house and Felix called Jean Paul to greet him and play with him and the child, when he approached him, kicking him with the orthopedic shoes he was wearing, hitting him on the shin, causing Felix to throw a cry of pain. And I also remembered when we went to visit Felicia, who gave him a boat-shaped radio, threw herself to the ground to play with him and the child hit her in the head with the bow of the radio ship that left her aunt stunned by the pain.

Robert had accepted Machin's proposal to rent the apartment and so we moved in again. At Machin Robert returned to buy him a refrigerator and a basket, thus making more expenses and engaging more and more. The house was narrower but I couldn't accept the life of disorder and bohemian that Robert wanted to live. Instead of rebelling, I gave myself to venting my anger by eating and, as a result of that, I started to gain more and more weight to the point that I myself realized that that skinny, agile girl I was no longer had the features of my face back then.

Between Robert and me there had been no love for a long time now; in me, perhaps there had never been.

There was a habit of living together and, sometimes they could months without making love.

Robert later started working at the Playboy Club in New York and came home late at night when I was already asleep. The days passed by, unless I received a letter from Yoohyeh, or if I had gone to visit my relatives. I'm not happy with anything and then I decided to do something for myself and go to the doctor to follow a diet to lose weight.

That's when we got a check from S.I.A.E., so Robert started plotting how to spend it may be buying a new car. I told him nothing because I knew it was useless, but because he liked to spend so much, I asked him: "Why don't you invest in a property or something like that could stay for our son tomorrow?"

To which Robert replied very coolly "I have lived like this for 46 years and now I will not change for anyone."

I felt tired of fighting with the man who had done what he wanted with money, not counting on me, that I had changed my life and that the least anticipated day would come for him to explode like a bomb.

Robert didn't wait long and when my anger subsided, he started looking for a car, finding a cougar, light yellow, and bought it without me. Summer arrived and Robert had still parked the Oldsmobile convertible without using it. One day the whole family agreed to go and eat a roast suckling pig in a picnic area on the seven-lake mountain.

Robert seemed to have sugar for the children:

Well, the day passed and everyone even enjoyed taking pictures to remember that moment of tranquility. Robert tried whenever he had the chance to call back the people he had met through Nino Tassone, and one day he met George Albert's president and cash box editor, who had good intentions about him and charged him with making arrangements for a girl named Stephanie, who repeatedly came home to try on the songs and George Gershwin's son also arrived.

A little bit about the diet and then the way people go into the house I got nervous and especially the piano and records that played, but I didn't say anything, it was summer and I had the baby with me. That morning I went to the park con Jean Paul who saw another guy who had a tricycle threw himself behind him to ride him. The boy did not want to lend it to him and Jean Paul grabbed him from behind the seat and the boy hastened to move away causing Jean Paul's hands to be freed and he fell to the floor causing one of his teeth to fall and blood to leak.

I picked it up from the ground and put the tooth in place with a slight pressure on the gum until the blood emptied and the tooth was a little out of place, but better than being without a tooth for a long time.

That incident infatuated Robert not because the boy had fallen but because he didn't like me putting his tooth forward- a little out of place. George Albert, who wanted to produce records with Robert suddenly, fell ill and doctors discovered that he had a very advanced cancer for which he died, so Robert's plans also died. He and his family are vacationing in Florida. When we arrived, I really liked Florida because the weather reminded me of Cuba. I was tired of the cold in New Jersey and New York. Robert then enjoyed the adventure, and taking an example from Caridad who had already moved to Boca Raton, we went to see her and told her that we would send him the money so that he would take care of taking an apartment so that- when he arrived with the move- we would have a place to live.

The holidays were best done by going to the beach, walking around Miami and its surroundings, eating even in Latin restaurants. Upon departure, everyone took their car on the way back. The journey lasted two and a half days, and my spine, suffered from the position so uncomfortable that avev or in that car so small that taking all the holes felt along the spine. When he got to the misi in bed, but I was not well at all and the next day raising my legs they could not reggerms because of the great pain. Robert took me to Dr. Richard Bosvalli, a chiropractic that with some sessions made me feel good.

Robert, meanwhile, began making plans to leave, but for the first time he was undecided about where he wanted to go because he knew that in Florida, he would have to start all over again and he didn't know anyone because he already had friends in the music field in New York where he had made his first musical arrangements. He talked to me about it, so I said,

"Robert, if I were you, I would go where I could work on what I know, and in your case it's music, because we don't go to California where you know people who can introduce you, for example Maurice Jarre whose address and phone you already have and you know that Franco Zefirelli does a lot of productions in Hollywood and you worked on the film he made with Elizabeth Taylor and Richard Burton The Timing of the *Shrew.*

And I continued, "Carlo Ponti also co-produces with America and you worked on the film *Once Upon a Time* with Sofia Loren and Omar Sharif and you also worked at the Lido in Paris with Dizzy Gillispie who is now here and can advise you."

But while I was talking or, I could see that Robert was only taken by his thoughts. Then he said:

"I'm going to talk to Mery, my agent, because I can write music wherever I want without having to go to California."

Some time passed and my brother, Giovanni, Irma, Iliana and Zuni, the two daughters, left for Miami, leaving me without any family members in New Jersey. The irony of fate... those relatives for whom we were in the United States were now 1500 miles from us.

Robert began to sell everything: the living room with the two tables, the lamps, and the portable washing machine. He wanted to be ready for when they left and knowing that I who could not or move me in that carso bassa and that almost no Avevor space behind, decis and to buy a station wagon that he had given in exchange for the Mercury Cougar as a down payment. He wanted me to see her but I replied:

I'm not well, leave me alone.

Robert insisted, "Dai, just a moment, nothing more."

I realized if I didn't go, she wouldn't leave me alone. Robert said to me:

"I'm going to take the car so it's closer when you get off."

And he rushed down the ladder as the boy and I descended more slowly, when suddenly I felt it turn my head and held me back on the ladder so as not to fall. The boy realized I was sick and asked me:

"What's mom?"

I would have liked to answer him and feci a gesture of the hand to tell him that it was nothing, but I felt the back of my head heavy and insensitive and - next to the neck- as if the blood was not flowing and the nerves in the mouth were stiff to the point that I could not speak. I thought it was just a moment and with my hand on the boy I tried to take another step on my legs that could no longer hold me and sat silently with the beating of his heart that looked like a horse on the run.

With a superhuman effort whispers to the boy "Call daddy!"

Jean Paul frightened ran to look for his father and when Robert arrived, I was breathing hard. Robert entered the house and called the doctor and also told him that I was on a diet but the doctor replied that she did not make any visits to the house and that she had to be transported to the hospital immediately and that to go faster she had to call the police so as not to waste time at the traffic lights she would find along the way.

Robert did this and within minutes, a police car appeared with two young officers, one with black hair that looked like they were of Italian origin and the other with light hair. They both asked Robert a few questions then turning to me they asked me if they should help me get in the car and whether he could or walk.

I said yes with a head movement and the officers helped me get up. Sapevor that I was walking but my mind was like a dream and I feel inert in the back of the police car resting my head in the seat. My vision was blurred and I could see very quickly the trees that seemed to want to touch the clouds.

When we arrived, a Cuban doctor immediately understood what was happening to me; he visited me and a few minutes later he went out and told Robert that the collapse that Avevor immediately was due to the drop in potassium that had lowered his blood pressure. He gave me an injection and said I'd be fine soon. I went home without seeing the car Robert wanted to buy because I thought it was also the discomfort of being forced to do something I didn't want that had caused me to collapse.

Robert, on the other hand, did not care and a few days after the accident, he appeared with the car at home, put a poster to Olds mobil to sell it and an advertisement in the newspaper, with good results. When the car was sold, he arrived home saying that his agent Mary had told him:

"Go to Florida, I have a job for you there, and while you enjoy the trip, go fishing that there is a lot of sea!"

I didn't resist anymore, I didn't care anything else, because I knew it was Robert who prepared everything.

She called a removal agency that made long trips and hired them to take everything to Boca Raton, Florida, where she had already sent Caridad the money to rent and an apartment near her.

Now we were ready, I took one last look at the apartment and we left in the station wagon.

The journey took place without incident, although it took us three days because we stopped many times and eventually reached boca raton moan.

Caridad and Félix lent us some things the first few days because the move was over. After the first few days of setting, I asked Robert "Well, and the work your agent would promise you, where is he?!"

Robert opened his blue eyes which were all he had ever given me and shrugging his shoulders replied

"I think I'm going to have to look for a job myself."

I couldn't believe it, once again he had deluded me or what he was saying was true. Comunque I had my IBM diploma and this time the child was at school all day, so I decided to take and an appointment with the head of the employees of the Hotel Boca Ratòno.

The next day I was called for a test, which went well and I started working in the hotel offices. Robert, on the other hand, tried to find work in his field to no avail and eventually made the decision to work as a security guard. And they were scared when she carried the gun, and put it on top of the closet for fear that Jean Paul l would get it.

It wasn't a month that we lived there and since that area was full of Atlantic University students who resided in those same apartments, one day one of them occupied the place in the driveway's Robert parking lot, which was assigned to each tenant: he parked, pulled out a bicycle from the trunk and started mounting. Robert reversed with the car and reached me as I said to the boy:

"Parking is ours and removes the car!"

The young man looked at me and ignored me cycling with his head very high as if he had not heard me, what angered Robert who parked the car and went in search of the young man who was already running so he could not reach him, the accident seemed to end there, but it was notso.

After a few hours walking along the waterfront, we saw the young man walking in their own direction, with hasty steps and trying to stop Robert from saying something to him but Robert invete:

"Hey you are rude! When a lady speaks to you the least you can do is answer her! Hey, I'm talking to you!"

The young man turned and said unrepeatable words, to which Robert reacted, ran to reach the young man, touched him from behind and said:

Are you going to answer me now? So, he slapped the young man who put himself in a karate position.

Robert leans back and points his open hand at the young man and says:

"It's clear you watch too much television. Fight like men!"

At the clamour several people came screaming and between them the director of the apartments that separated them.

In the evening around 7 a.m. they knocked on the door, it was the police that the boy had called to report the attack he had suffered from Robert. The officer told Robert:

"I look like good people atheist, these students have hot heads, if I were you, I would move or buy a house in a better place, especially for your son."

Robert muttered a few words of apology and told the officer that he had also thought that in the future, not too far away, he intended to move. The policeman said good night and left because the boy had not filed a complaint against us. Robert kept thinking and said,

You know buying a house wouldn't be a bad idea! – I didn't say anything...

After a month of that incident Robert came home excited because he had found work in an Italian restaurant in Ft. Lauderdale, called Davinci, and was well paid. I, on the other hand, Avevor received a salary increase because avev or more responsibility, in managing the entire hotel and together with another woman took care of us mor to make the computer work. It looked like everything was going well until one day I got that damn back pain back. Eror at home waiting for it to pass, but it was in vain why he decided to go to the chiropractor, who advised me to rest and lose weight to get better.

I began the diet that the doctor had prescribed me, with good results; the first month I lost 14 kilos and felt better because I kept taking the vitamins that the doctor had ordered. One day Robert says to me:

"You know the restaurant owner throws a party at his house to celebrate his birthday and wants us to go, I play the piano, come on, have fun."

At the party I didn't know anyone; I sit down to watch Robert play. Land women approached him as if he had honey because of how well he sounded by asking him for pieces that were their favorites. Dared to spend the night, finally at dawn we took the car and went home. Robert was flattering me that night, perhaps thinking of some of the women who had charmed him while he was playing, and he thinks that he behaved a little strangely, so much so that when he went to bed, he threw himself on me to eat me with kisses, which he had never done and d being alone in the flat home, with a few drinks we bonded in the passion of the night.

Jean Paul's birthday came on November 25 to coincide with the Thanksgiving celebration. We celebrated with the whole family because Giovanni, Irma and the two girls had come from Miami for the occasion and Avevor reserved the news for that moment. Everyone was happy because Jean Paul would have a little brother or sister.

I wasn't entirely sure I wanted to, and I talked to Robert

"You know what the doctor told me? As long as you rest, take a long journey to lose it naturally.

What do you think?"

You know I like kids and a company for Jean Paul would be good for him.

"Since I don't work anymore, I could have the baby."

In the following week we went looking for a house in Miami to no avail, but the second time we took the ring road and went down to Calder Race Track. None had traveled that for a few blocks when suddenly ads of houses appeared for sale. We walked into a place called Cherry Bay. The house salesman was a man a little older than Robert and as a very attentive salesman, he showed us several apartments, obviously they were decorated very well and I liked them. Robert then said to the man:

"Beh now shows me what he has for sale. And we went to see him."

I asked Robert, "Are you sure you want to buy that house?"

Robert had already purchased a money order for the amount requested, and handed it over to the man who had given him a receipt and said that we had to come back the next day to sign all the other documents necessary for the purchase and so it happened.

The month of December passed slowly, it seemed that the days would never end, so much was the anxiety to move into the new house we had, and when we realized that Christmas was about to arrive, preparations began and Caridad decided to celebrate it at his house on December 24.

That day we met all and the gifts were exchanged, having fun in what was due to Felix's drunkenness. **(I WOULD DELETE THIS SONG,** in incomprehensible red AND NOT USEFUL FOR THESTORY), which every time there was a party gave the note trying to raise the horn of Irma **or Felicia because it was Caridad or Bella did not pay attention to him, they already knew him well and he didn't know He dared not say anything to John because once they had to go to his hands for the same thing, and of** course he respected Robert because he had not had much knowledge with him, so he looked for the two who paid the most attention to him and got angry, if it wasn't for that, everything would have gone well.

I was already two months pregnant when we moved into Miami's new home. John helped him move, without knowing that the doctor had told me to be quiet until three months had passed.

Everything looked much well in the new house: there was lighter and more space outside, while Robert, if he had stayed at home, he could have spent time watching TV with Jean Paul on his way home from school.

One day we invited Giovanni, his wife and the girls to come and eat with us. Jean Paul and Zuni, the youngest of the girls, always quarreled for one reason or another. At one point they walked into the closet and dropped a door with such a big noise that I ran scared and when I saw the door on the ground you start arguing with Irma blaming her for letting the girls do what they wanted. One word pulls the other until Irma told John that she was picking up her things and that she would never come again.

When they left, I scolded Jean Paul and Robert and sat him on his legs like a child and said:

"You shouldn't have blamed him. - And then turned to Jean Paul: - Not listening to mom who's crazy!"

From that day I began to observe Robert how he behaved with Jean Paul towards me. He was putting the baby against me. And when I punished him for educating him, Robert consoled him by saying,

"Mom's bad, don't listen to her." That put me in a bad mood, and I was trying to control myself because I knew he was hurting the unborn child, too.

One day we got a letter from Robert's mother, who wrote that they were coming.

all to spend a few days of vacation and would stay at our house not to spend much in the hotel and to stay longer because they came from France and the trip would have been expensive. Well Robert was happy because he would see his family, especially his mother. He went into orbit and bought sofas-bed. Robert's sister Simone Derepp and husband Jean slept in the living room, on the other hand Robert's mother slept with Jean Paul in his room.

They were all happy to wait for another baby.

"I'm sorry, but I don't think I'm going to see it." Robert's mother said because she wasn't feeling very well. The days passed with guests at home and each time went more everyone, to the beach, to the zoo or jungle park or where Robert played. We went to eat fried chicken in a Kentucky Fried Chicken.

Jean Paul, after eating, no longer wanted to sit at the table and began to walk between the places of the restaurant which was almost empty and in my carelessness, he knows jumping from place to place by incorrectly. Calculating the distance and falling over the iron armor surrounding the seats and, with the iron angle caused by a deep wound in his left eyebrow. To the cry of the child brings him to the table by buffering the wound so that he did not bleed so much. I had a moment of anger to see grandma's indifference to my son as the blood did not stagnate and thought it was necessary to give points, while grandma did not move.

We finally went to the hospital where the doctor put seven stitches on his eyebrow.

Robert's mother soon said she wanted to leave and was escorted to the airport. We greeted each other at home because Jean Paul had not yet returned from school and I had to wait for him. When he left, he stood and looked at me and, in my nod of greeting, I saw in his gaze a farewell forever. I never saw her again.

Kenneth

Robert had befriended neighbors next door and among them with what he called the youngest of them who was 29 years old and worked at National Airlines. His name was Kenneth School and he went to war in Vietnam, Korea and Laos. His father and older brother lived with him. One day Robert saw that Kenneth had a machine to cut the grass and asked to borrow. Kenneth replied:

"Let me cut your weed for you."

And since then, Robert hasn't cut the grass and invites him to eat, to go out with them. That friendship bothered me because I didn't like to abuse the kindness of neighbors, but I didn't say anything or anything because Kenneth did it spontaneously.

Robert's singing friend Aldo Landi proposed to Robert to create a recording studio and he agreed and signed up a plan to put it in the house. One afternoon- after Jean Paul arrived from school- he asked permission to go and play ball in the park near the house, permission was given and he ran where friends were already waiting for him.

It didn't take long for a group of guys to arrive running and screaming, one of whom was twice as tall as Jean Paul. When I went out, I had one of the most unpleasant surprises of life. Jean Paul had been hit by that boy and held his head and the same eye where he had received the stitches before.

But this time he had been shot under the eyebrow. A deep wound showed the flesh of the eye giving the impression that it was the eye that was injured.

The fear was so great that I put my hands on my eyes so as not to see and fell almost eventually. Robert who followed me supported me so that it did not fall even for my state of gestation so advanced. Con the boy who hit Jean Paul went to the nearest hospital.

The boy is paler than ever, explained that he had Jean Paul behind him and when he hit him, with the baseball bat, with all his strength, he did not realize that the boy was very close to him. After the statements were compiled and the points were given to Jean Paul, all four of us returned home, leaving the boy in his, not far from us.

The days passed and I was in my eighth month of pregnancy when Robert thought about changing and driving in a Ford Comet after the station wagon, he had brought from New Jersey. Thinking, as always about the future, I said to him, "We have not yet finished paying for the car we have and you are already buying another one!"

"He thinks I have to give birth next month, and you're making a lot of international calls in Italy and that's going to cost you more than you think."

I was right, Robert and Aldo were planning to go to Italy to record the album and spent hours on the phone planning everything for the trip to Rome.

A fortnight later, Robert had everything ready for his departure and greeted Kenneth by telling me to keep everything ready by the time it was time to go to the hospital. He would come back in time from the trip after ten days. Kenneth, at that time, would help me and see me every day after work to see if anything was needed or if she was okay. One day he was joking with me about my belly, which was quite big, and he said to me: "Maybe you have two in the oven!"

And I said, "Don't worry, the doctor says he's one, and besides, you don't want to be a godfather for two? Then remember you told me you were going to baptize the baby!"

On his return Robert came with me, for the last medical examination, before giving birth and Dr. Theodor Leher confirmed what he already knew or, that he would have given birth to him. Orra I just had to choose the day. Think of the alfour July, which is a national holiday throughout the United States, but the doctor admitted that, since it was a national holiday, there would be no staff in the hospital, if you had complications during the operation, and that it was better not to take any risks.

So, we agreed on July 2, 1974 and, in the hospital of Mount Sinai, a girl of seven and a half kilos was born with a height of 21 inches and we called her Jessica Michelle Poitiven.

Robert was very happy with the birth of the baby and called my whole family, including Giovanni and Irma. I didn't know or very well after giving birth, he had lost a lot of blood and when I woke up from anesthesia, Dr. Leher said to me:

"You won't be able to have more children, another could cost your life, you've lost a lot of blood and you're safe, think about recovering that you have a beautiful little girl."

After the birth of the baby, I didn't want children anymore, nor did Robert, observing how Jean Paul was growing up and even one day I had in mind to separate from my husband.

I was in the hospital for 10 days and Robert didn't have all the money to pay the bill or insurance, but he didn't tell me anything until I left the hospital. She was out of work and without money because she had spent it on the trip to Italy and had recorded the album done, to no avail. She didn't have anyone to distribute it to her, so it was a waste of time and money. What he did was put another drop of water in a glass that had been full for a long time. When I left the hospital, sore from the wound, I was forced to do everything in the house; Robert only took care of Jean Paul and tried to cover up debts by secretly selling even what he managed to take away without seeing him. He took my mink and when I realized it was missing, he found a stupid excuse. And the fur doesn't see it anymore.

And one day came the final phone bill, with a note saying, to pay immediately or the telephone service would be disconnected. The bill was $400. We had a bad fight and I said,

"Before you made the phone calls in Italy, I told you it would cost you a lot and now the amount is so big that no one can pay it. Why don't you tell Aldo to pay at least half? Aren't you partners?"

But the days passed and Aldo paid nothing and we were left without a phone. The company with which they rented the plan picked him up for lack of payment. It had only been 18 days since childbirth and I was still feeling weak. Everything that was happening hit my nerves a lot, gradually seeing that everything I owned or was sold; Robert was out of work and now with two children.

That day, Robert found an ad of who bought used furniture, called, and the buyer offered $150 for the set of rooms we bought in New Jersey for a thousand dollars. Feci sign Robert not to accept and bargain. Then the man concluded, "Okay, 200 with mattresses." And Robert agreed.

I was very depressed; I went to the kitchen to make milk for the little girl and tears flowed down my cheeks without me being able to control them. Pensavo "Care it be of me with the children if I separate from Robert?" Would I have found a reliable person to leave the baby to? And what kind of work would I find to support myself and the children?

With these thoughts in mind, when Robert came in and saw me crying, he didn't even look at him and that Kenneth came in and noticed that he was going to have to cry and then looked at Robert as if he were looking for an answer, so he invited him out to the patio to talk to him. After a few minutes they came back and Robert said to me:

"I have to go to Miami Beach. I have a business appointment; if you need anything, Kenneth will be home today because it's his day off." And having said that, he left without first taking the book of Gregorian Chants of 1443 that I had brought from Italy and without me seeing him.

Kenneth tried to comfort me by telling me "It's not worth crying for anyone else; an attractive woman like you can make everyman happy."

That said, he took a hand in his and stroked it with intensity. His eyes were fixed in the void looking through the window but without seeing anything; it was as if his thought was far from there. I noticed that he didn't realize what he was doing and called him to wake him up from a dream.

"Kenneth, Kenneth!"

She was shaking my hand too much, and then let her go. What were you thinking? I asked him.

"You reminded me of someone I met when I was at war..."

And after a pause he added:

"These are the symptoms of those who fought."

Then he fell silent as if he didn't want to finish the sentence.

"What specialty did you have at war?"

And he no longer spoke because he had touched a conversation that he could not hear about and with an excuse that I had to go home, he just said to me:

"Yes, and you need me to call me, okay? Oh, for what you asked me, I was in the artillery."

"I was thoughtful. Yes, and offended by my curiosity?" But without thinking about it, I shrugged my shoulders and continued to look after the little girl who had fallen asleep after taking milk. I looked at me and said,

"To think I didn't want to have you! And now I'm not changing you at all; you will be different from your brother, you do not give me any problem, angel of God!"

When the sun lurked behind the horizon and you could see it through the clouds, with an orange color, and formed some drawings in the sky, with the little girl in the car sitting in front of my house watching Jean Paul ride a bike when Robert arrived with the news that he had found work as a pianist at the Azteca hotel in Miami Beach located on Collins Avenue.

Kenneth, who was sitting inside his house and looking out the living room window, also saw that Robert had arrived and went out to greet him and tell him that everything was fine referring to me. We all walked into the house, I went to put the little girl to bed so that she could talk to Robert and have more details about the work she was talking about. We sat at the dining room table and Robert began to tell of the audition he had done so for which they had accepted it immediately and the salary with weekly payments, was enough for the 1970s.

He then took a roll of banknotes from the roll and put it in front of Bella saying that he had done business with the book he had taken.

What book? I asked him.

Well, what we had there.

Seeing the void where the book normally was, I said nothing else, got up and walked out of the room.

When I went down the hallway, I realized my legs weren't holding me and I grabbed the wall so I wouldn't fall. Robert looked at me and so did Kenneth; the two ran at the same time taking me by the arms and carrying me they asked me, "What have you got?"

I felt pain in my left arm, which took my hand numbing my **fingers**.

It was as if my nerves were not responding and when I wanted to or speaks to answer then ask, I could not or; the tongue was heavy and the words came out inconsistent, the heart was beating hard and it looked cold. I heard everything around and feci sign to bring me a pencil and a sheet of paper: Robert knew where to look for it and brought them to me.

I wrote with difficulty that Avevor cold, and even if they covered me, felt or a strange frost from the feet and salivated on the thighs and hands, which were frosty. It was a heat crisis and it had been going on for hours and Robert didn't call a doctor or ambulance to take me to the hospital. The night was coming and Kenneth, he came back to see how I was, discovering that Robert had done nothing for me and that my condition had worsened.

He began to walk around the room wiping sweat from his forehead. She didn't know how to tell Robert that she had to call someone until, with a groan; he showed him a sign to approach, telling him with a breath of voice that I could not take it anymore and that she called the ambulance to be taken to the hospital.

So, Kenneth called Robert and told him that, it was his responsibility, as my husband and that he had to do it and that if he did, he would make him responsible for what might have happened.

Robert saw that Kenneth was so determined he called the emergency room that, he arrived early and Kenneth ran to show where my house was. Within minutes the nurses prepared me for the ambulance ride and Robert left Jean Paul at Kenneth's and called the ambulance.

When I arrived at North Medical Center at 27th Avenue and 147th Street they immediately took me to the emergency room where there were two nurses who took care of me until the doctor arrived. The nurses tried to check the sensitivity of the feet, but without results, they gave up.

Then Dr. Burn finally arrived, took a look at what the paramedics had written and also found that it was more serious than they had thought. He tried to talk to me, but he could not or answer him.

In spite of all this, I have not lost consciousness; or aware of everything around me but nothing else, so Dr. Burn gave me an injection and went to talk to Robert who was waiting outside the emergency room telling him that with the injection I would fall asleep all night and that in the morning I was able to talk and feel better.

The doctor left and Robert, with the help of the nurses, took me to the car, heading to the house where Kenneth was waiting for us and when he saw us arrive, carefully, he took me by the arm and Robert on the other, taking me to the house where they put me to bed, closing the door behind them.

The next morning, I woke up when Robert had already returned from taking Jean Paul to school and asked him:

"What time is it?" And jump out of bed worried about the kids. Robert reassured me that he had already taken Jean Paul to school and the little girl had taken the milk. Either what I had to do was dress up to see Dr. Burn with whom he had more a date for that day in the morning.

Once we were in the office, the doctor asked me to come in without my husband because he wanted to talk to me alone. When I was in the office, the doctor also let the nurse out and told her to close the door and began reading aloud the report about her from the previous night, asking me if she knew or what all that meant. The answer is as to:

'You should explain it to me. I don't know the medical terminology and I don't know anything about it."

So, the doctor, who until then, had stayed on his feet, took a wheelchair and sat down to get comfortable and listen to what I was going to say.

He began by asking me what was wrong with me putting me in this terrible state like when I got to the emergency room the night before.

"It's all because of the family situation, and because of that, I can't control my nerves anymore. There were too many things I had to endure in ten years of marriage."

The doctor looked at me and asked me, "How old are you?"

"Thirty-one, Doctor..."

He answered by staring at me "Sand you don't solve your problem very soon you won't see the 32-year-old. This is advice from doctor to patient; you can do whatever you want. To prescribe these pills that will calm you down, you will only take them at night only if you do not go out because they will make you very sleepy, but remember the pills are not the ones that will cure you, it is you who have to remove the problems that hurt you so much."

The doctor said nothing else and I knew or that he was telling me the truth. I said yes, that he was right and that he wanted to live many more years to see my children grow up.

Dr. Burn got up and shook my hand smiling sadly. When I got out, Robert asked me in the car:

"Well... and what did the doctor tell you?"

I answered vaguely and a little dry, without letting him know exactly what the doctor had told me. I just showed him the prescription of the pills and told him they had to go buy them and before they went home. Then, I did not say another word, while the car ran disappearing among others that disappeared, who knows where, like my many thoughts.

From that day I had to go to the hospital, the relationship between Robert and me was no longer the same as before. I was slowly recovering from the collapse and thinking "I'm the mother of his children, I left a career that was already at its peak, I gave him the best years of my life and he, he wasn't even calling the ambulance and he was going to let me die."

And I was reminded of scenes from my own movies... THIS WOULD BE FINE IN ANY FILM REPRESENTATION

I also wanted to baptize the little girl before I put into practice what I wanted to do with that wedding. Kenneth had already told me that she wanted to be the godfather; the godmother would be Michelle, Robert's niece of whom Jessica Michelle bore her name. Baptism took place in the Catholic Church of Santa Monica.

Michelle had not been able to make the trip from France to Miami and replaced her sister-in-law, Irma.

There was also my brother Giovanni and the two daughters with my two sisters who, for the occasion came from West Palm Beach bringing with them a couple of friends from Caridad and Félix, her husband. Irma's cousin Ana and her husband and their three children, with whom Jean Paul liked to play, were present at the reception.

It all took place in a familiar and joy-filled atmosphere and, after lunch, danced and when everyone was tired, they asked Robert to play some pieces with the accordion he had in the house. At night the party vanished and the first to leave were my sisters because they had to go a long way. Then everyone left.

I put the little girl to sleep thinking "Thank God, I baptized her!" It wasn't long before things got complicated again. One morning came the man Robert had ordered the fence to be arranged in the back of the patio, so that Jean Paul would play without danger of going to the street. I knew how to apologize for not paying, and he almost insulted me and threatened to remove the fence and take it away.

I told him to talk to my husband and tell him when Robert would be home. In fact, at the agreed time Robert had already arrived and the man did not wait, immediately got to the point and gave him three days to pay. Then he turned his back on Robert and left.

"So, Robert asked me, "Why did you tell him when I was coming back?"

You can't take it anymore. It came out everything that was kept in me for ten years and, for the first time, I told him about the divorce, and that I didn't have to give him or anything else to give him for him to sell. It reminds him of everything he had taken from me including Canti Gregorian's book, of inestimable value, which was the last thing he had brought with him.

The next morning, Robert and I went to downtown Miami to find a lawyer and to the courthouse to ask for information, and there they provided the address of attorney Abner Solomon. When we took the elevator, neither of us said a word.

The lawyer was tall and thin, with slightly gray hair peeing from his temples. His voice struck me: it was a sweet and calm voice that inducing confidence and relaxation, almost total, when you were in his presence, and this is how I felt or and thought: "Finally my suffering with this man will end."

Poor I, if you knew that from that first step towards divorce with Robert, everything would not have been as you though tor, and that from then on, the suffering would become even greater.

After presenting the case to the lawyer and having found that the divorce took place by mutual agreement, he requested $400 for his services. I was determined to put an end to that situation, so I don't think twice about it and took the money Robert gave me- for the week's groceries- by giving the lawyer an advance to start preparing the papers.

Robert looked at me and it seemed as if for the first time he understood that he was determined to do everything, followed with his gaze the money he was giving or giving to Abner Solomon, but said nothing. He ignores him and doesn't even remarry those looks of his.

While we were in the car, I was alone with my thoughts: Quello that avev or accumulated inside me for all those 10 years, had reached the end and nothing would disturb or that great sense of freedom: feel or walk inside the clouds; it was a difficult feeling to explain, but I didn't think about the sad consequences that divorce would have on me and my children.

When we got home, I went to Kenneth's house where I had or left the baby to his father, and now holding her in my arms I went to the living room to see me by the window she gave on the back patio. Robert, who had begun to collect her clothes to leave the house, seeing the little girl in my arms, approached her talking to her and me at the same time:

"And to think that I believed that the birth of the child would consolidate our marriage but I see that I was wrong!"

Having said that, he took my hand to ask me to give him another chance, that things would be fixed, but I was now determined not to go back, and I remembered that if it wasn't for Kenneth, he would let me die without calling the ambulance, and what the doctor had also told me:

"If you don't solve the problem, you won't get to see the 32-year-old."

Everything had occurred to me in a second and, after he had spoken to me, I took my hand out of his and Robert no longer insisted; took the portable turntable saying:

"Well, I need one, and you're going to have to find another one to listen to the album Kenneth gave you for your comp."

There was a tone of jealousy in his voice that I had never heard in him. When she finished collecting her belongings, she left, giving the little girl a kiss saying to me:

Tell Jean Paul, I'll come and see him as soon as I settle down at Aldo's house.

After Robert left, my life unfolded around the children. I took Jean Paul to school in the morning on foot so as not to waste gas, I took care of the house and the girl at the same time until I went to pick up the boy at school. For food errands, wait until Kenneth was home to help me load them up from the supermarket, leaving the little girl with her father who liked to take her on arms or reminding her of the little girl her eldest son had had with a South American who didn't even bring him closer, so he was proud to take care of Jessica so that I could buy what he had or needed.

Almost every week Robert came to bring me money for food and to see the kids, but payments for the house and car were not taken into account. Unfortunately, he didn't know the laws and didn't have a lawyer or money to pay for one. Meanwhile Kenneth didn't miss an opportunity to win me over, under the guise of seeing the little girl and if he had anything or needed something he never said no.

One day precisely he was cutting the grass and I went to bring him a glass of iced tea that he had learned to drink while fighting in Vietnam, Korea and Laos. So, he took advantage of that moment that he had turned off the lawnmower to say "I have to talk to you seriously." And, after drinking, here turn the glass to my hands with intensity, and I imagined what he wanted to tell me. Kenneth immediately got to the point and said,

"You know there's nothing I don't do for you, and knowing your situation and the kind of woman you are, even as a mother..." There was a short pause as if weighing the words and, in the end,, he said:

"What I want to tell you is that I'm in love with you."

He took my hands to continue: "I can help you with Jean Paul and I am also Michelle's godfather, but we have to take care of my father, you know it would always be an example for children."

But I didn't let him finish. Sapevor what I needed and all the financial problems that Avevor, videte skies open and without thinking anymore, immediately replied yes.

Kenneth's eyes lit up, he got up and- without letting go of my hands- he gave me a kiss as a symbol of the pact he had or just made. I realized I had to go to work or have other help, because that way I couldn't move on. I got all the bills from the house and the car and I couldn't pay them, I was in a vicious circle. On the one hand, Robert didn't give me more than to eat, and the little girl needed a woman to take care of her, if I had to work - and where I lived, I couldn't find anyone available among the neighbors, nor could I leave her to Kenneth's father for eight hours, besides the fact that the old man liked to drink a lot of wine, and if holding her he dropped it?

I had tried in every way to ask for help and having no money to pay the lawyer, the divorce had remained in the legal separation. And just for that reason, when she went to ask for government help, they denied it to me, making it clear that I would have to bring divorce papers, and without them they couldn't help me.

It was a time when I had acted without thinking too much about it, to get out of a financial situation that could not be more serious. I was still writing to Yoohyeh and asked him to come to America, now that I was legally separated from my husband, but he took a long time to respond to my letters and when he did, he always had a new movie to make or some business tied him to Rome.

She told me how much she loved me and that she had never forgotten me, that she was alone with memories of her, but that she had to wait for the visa to be issued or that someone from her family who had California could call him back. He said to me: -- It doesn't take long. But the time to wait was what I didn't know.

What I didn't know was that by leaving my house, there was a risk of losing it at the time of the divorce. The next day, he published a notice in the paper to rent the house, and at the same time rented an apartment in Hialeah as I had decided with Kenneth and my sister-in-law.

After making the announcement in the papers, since i didn't have a phone inthe house, call the Irmas from the street to invite her for that Sunday with my nieces and brother, to which Irma replied:

"Look at the coincidence that Ana came to see me this Sunday! So, we're all coming?"

I said yes, but not without thinking that, every time she was invited, she had to carry someone else behind like the dog's tail. When Sunday arrived, the lunch I had prepared was a dish I had learned in Italy: spaghetti carbonara with bacon, eggs and grated Parmesan cheese; it's a delicious dish and doesn't cost much time or money to prepare.

After eating and drinking from a bottle of wine, brought by Kenneth, the boys went to the yard to play while the older ones stayed to talk congratulating me on what I would do, moving with Kenneth to Hialeah. They said,

At least you won't be alone and you'll be close to your brother.

The conversation had been very pleasant when someone knocked on the door. I went to see who he was and when I opened; I saw a man and a woman with a boy about thirteen years old who wanted to see the house.

The woman was of medium stature, sporty, dressed in white pants and a sweater, brown hair collected, while her husband had white shorts as a tennis player; his hair and eyes were black, thus denouncing his Italian origin, his thirteen-year-old son, had the same body as his father and for as long as they stayed there, he did not say a word.

The house interested them and they wanted to make a contract right away because they lived in a hotel and the furniture was in a warehouse. I gave them a receipt for $600 dollars, they gave me the money and the deal were done. They claimed that they would move the following weekend, thus giving me time to move.

The couple and their son greeted with a handshake and left. He stayed with my family to celebrate what happened. Now Avevor money to move me but, there was something in those people that I couldn't perceive, couldn't or do without noticing it and I was right to doubt. What I had agreed at that time I would suffer it later. That couple who didn't smile wouldn't bring anything good. With Kenneth we moved to Hialeah. After the move I became interested in who could take care of the child and found an

Elderly lady living in the building with her single daughter; the lady agreed to take care of the little girl so I could look for a job.

When I got home that day, I already had a job at Allied Leisure Inc. Industry. It was early May and in Florida the days were wonderful. Jean Paul was picked up in the morning and taken home in the afternoon with the same school bus he paid for or weekly. Kenneth always worked with the national airline, earning little but with what I earned and that Robert passed on to the boys, we were fine.

The days spent like that and the biggest fun was the weekend when we went to the park for a picnic or bike, or to the beach when the good season came. We also took advantage of the pool of the building where my nieces sometimes came. I didn't like going swimming in the pool, I prefer the beach and I liked watching from the balcony when Kenneth and Jean Paul were playing the ball.

Everything seemed to be going well. I continued to follow the diet and you could already see the results. And I was just fine with 30 kilos less. One day told me that he worked on a passenger ship called Bohemia, that he and Aldo Landi played, which was better for him, because living on Bohemia he didn't have to pay for either home or food.

Meanwhile, I was realizing, after a year of living with Kenneth, that I was the main financial backer of the house that Kenneth partially contributed to and that I was keeping alone, and in my eyes, he was already letting me down. Then, the house I Avevor rented, to the couple who did not smile, gave me trouble. I thought Robert paid the monthly fee to the company with which he had or financed at home, but that was not the case and I received a letter from the owner.

When I went to the lawyer, he told me that he had to live in the house in order to force Robert to pay or otherwise he would lose all the rights to the house. With Kenneth we went to see the tenants and told them that we would return the money from the fund they had given him. But we found that they had moved in and had taken everything that belonged to me - the kitchen, the fridge, the dishwasher and the air conditioner- and this seemed little in front of the fact that they had filled the carpets with black earth.

I later put the house up for sale because I didn't have the money to buy all the stolen electrical effects. The lady who cared for Michelle moved to another part of Hialeah, not far from us, and so I moved too to be closer to her in the Pen-Mer Apts apartments and it was September 1975.

At the end of the year Robert tried to come back to me and invited us to spend a week of vacation, that Christmas and New Year on the ship Bohemia where he worked. We went there without Kenneth and had a great time visiting Puerto Plata, Puerto Prince and San Tomas with its Pineapple Bay and cobblestone streets reminding me of the old streets of Europe.

At the end of the tour, we agreed to take an apartment and since I didn't want to have any relationship with Robert, I spoke to Kenneth and as he didn't care anything and since everyone had his own room, we moved to 1287 NE on 118th Street, the neighbors were a bit of everything. There was a Canadian married to an American who once took a few more drinks and painted the dog's paws- named Suzy- with pink paint because he said it was female.

With this couple Robert befriended, the man naturally spoke French and they understood each other well. One day the neighbor gave a party so that Robert could hear his son playing in a rock band. After all the instruments were assembled and ready to play Robert came out dressed and scented because he was going to see someone and didn't have time to listen to the guy play. The other neighbor who was a priest of a Catholic church went to and take what we had bought for the party and discovered that I Avevor her husband, with whom he did not have or still divorced, and the friend who lived together in the same house.

I enrolled Jean Paul in a school that was close to our house, and showed him the way back in the afternoon along with the other kids who made the same way.

One day when the child who was about 9 years old and was strong in build and tall for his age was expected by two girls, thirteen and fourteen years old, who lived nearby with his mother who worked at night in a restaurant. Well, they were waiting for him and they started asking him if he wanted to have sex with them. The boy told them no. Then they began to hit Jean Paul who came home crying and bruised by the blows he had received. And after explaining to me what had happened, I didn't think twice and confronted the girl and so that the girl could give me an explanation of what they had done to my son. I was angry and she thought how those little girls dared to prick him with the thorns of the grass and also offer him sex, as if he were a man. In those thoughts my gaze fell on a piece of pipe used for plumbing and abandoned there. I picked him up from the ground, a few steps away was the girl who when he saw me stiffened.

I asked him, "Why did you hit my son?"

"I don't know, and what does it matter!" The girl then raised her hand to push me and at the same time saying:

"Get out of the way!" More enraged than ever with that girl who was my own height, almost a woman who cared nothing about what she had done, I said:

"Listen carefully! I'm going to see my son go away-don't look at him -don't approach him and don't talk to him, because if you don't, you're going to have serious problems with me."

You can't do anything to me. "You marry me laughing. Since I'm smaller..."

I shook hands on the tube I had picked up and lifted it forcefully and dropped it on the girl's thigh, which at the same time contracted and her lips rippled with pain, while I lifted the tube again threatening her that I would give it to her if she didn't leave my son alone.

"Do you understand!?"

The girl who massaged her thigh was paralyzed by fear and said yes with a movement of the head.

I went home. I knew those girls weren't from a good family and maybe I was afraid of the reactions. Kenneth hadn't come home from work and Robert was gone. In fact, with the sunset, they knocked on the kitchen door, it was the girls' mother who wanted an explanation. I told her what had happened but the woman threatened me that she would call or the police because the girls were minors.

I replied, "And my son is not even younger than them? You're not going to do anything against me because I'm going to tell you that men come in and out of your house at night when you go to work and you smell marijuana coming out of your house. Your girls set a bad example to the minors who live in the neighborhood. Ah! I forgot that the owner comes to see the apartment as it is full of graffiti of all the colors of the rainbow. Do you dare to think so? Chiama if you want the police."

The woman and the two girls gasped without being able to say anything, and left. Soon after I heard a noise in the kitchen window, I went to see what was going on and found that they had peed and spat in a plastic bottle and threw it in the kitchen.

I told the children to go into the room and close the door; the children obeyed and took dirty panties of the little girl, crossed the narrow corridor of grass that separated the two houses, and stuck the honeycomb... to the door handled and the insolent neighbors and back to the home closing the door behind me.

When one of them arrived, he screamed "Guarda! Non we can open door... the handle is full of excrement. Ah, that doesn't end there! -- And they knocked on my door again. To prii with a machete in their hand saying to them: - You urinated; spat d in the windows and, well, that's my answer!"

The woman came forward as if to attack and I put forward the machete taking it with both hands as I told her:

"It's self-defense and sand come in, I'll cut you off!"

Bluffed but I said it so well that the three women pulled back, turned around and left, not without before I was told one last word of insult. I closed the door with a sigh of relief. Learning to act now had really served.

A Priest A Little ... Strange

It seems like I didn't have to find peace where I had moved, and one afternoon, which was September Jean Paul came back from school when another guy started insulting him and our family with unrepeatable words and it wasn't the first time he did. Then Jean Paul, to defend his honor and that of his family, began to fight with that boy, in the same street, in front of the house of the reverend Ted, the latter told them that if they did not stop, he would call the police. Jean Paul came home and told me what had happened.

I couldn't imagine the priest being serious about his threats and I told my son that he seemed worried:

"If it's really serious, the reverend will come and talk to me, not be afraid; he just wanted to scare you."

Instead, fifteen minutes later there was a police car with two officers, who were more benevolent and understanding than the reverend himself. I told them that the priest had behaved very meanly, that reproaching the boy and coming to talk to me that he was the mother and also, that he should be ashamed to make so many stories with a 10-year-old boy and stop gossiping with neighbors and also have parties with loud music at 2 or 3 in the morning, and finally that the next time he disturbs the peace of neighbors I would call the police.

The cops, seeing that they had no reason to be there, greeted him and left. But the Reverend was furious at failing to punish the child, and entered his house to write me a letter threatening that civil law would lead her to put my son in a juvenile reformatory.

When I read the letter, I ripped it into a thousand pieces for the disgust it felt, and began to think that this was due to the fact that I had removed Jean Paul from the catechism. Dovevor do it as Father Ted practiced ragazz the ambiguous. Her hair that used to be black was now blonde. I didn't care much about this but the thing that made me decide was when I noticed the visitors to the house who were young people with homosexual tendencies and reputations, like him who even standing, in front of the house, sunbathed in a bikini. All passers-by could do nothing but look at him almost naked, and not to mention the late-night parties and with the Juke Box as loud turntables.

So, I thought "What happened with the two girls next door and the Canadian neighbor, all these people turned against me because they're of a different race and they don't want me here! Ah, but it's not. Now I will write a letter to Pope Paul VI, telling him everything reverend Theodor Sherwood does."

The letter to the Pope read as follows:

> By your eminence, you're Excellency, Pope
> Paul VI.
>
> Pontiff of St. Peter's Basilica in Vatican City.
>
> We kiss your hands and ask for her blessing,
> me Alicia Poitevin and my family, my son
> Jean Paul of 10 years and my daughter

Jessica M. of 3 years, as well as my husband Robert Poitevin.

Dear Eminence, this is to do you justice not only for my son, Jean Paul, but also for the Catholic Church. The dominant problem is one of your church representatives, Rev. Dr. Theodore "Ted Sherwood" resident at 1295 NE 118 Street, North Miami, Florida 33169, St. Peter Rectory.

After that I set out in detail the events that took place and set out my considerations:

The Reverend would have done better, in my opinion if he had lectured the child and come to me, his mother, but no, he did very badly. I decided to write this letter because if all the representatives of the Catholic and non-Catholic Church behaved as severely as "the rotten apple" in a barrel of good apples, that if it were not removed it would ruin all the other and …

Here I will give you the report on the end of the school year that my son finished last year. As you might see this is the name of the school and the address in case you want to investigate, but first I think it would be appropriate to investigate the morality of Father Ted, so he called the aforementioned reverend. The fact is that I had Jean Paul study catechism with Father Ted and had to remove it because apart from the fact that the reverend presents himself as a somewhat ambiguous guy, with blond-dyed hair that used to be black" and visitors are all teenagers with gay tendencies and reputation. To give you a clear picture of this reverend's person, I'll tell you that he sunbathes in a bikini in front of his house in a street where everyone who passes by car or on foot sees him. Almost naked, his body is exposed to passers-by. The parties he holds in his house, which would be the rectory, are made with music of all kinds contained in a juke-box and last until two or three in the morning, without any consideration for neighbors who cannot sleep and the next morning they have to go to work.

Another thing, he goes to the neighbors' house to hear the slander and gossip against me just because I'm natin Cuba, and I'm not of their race. Unfortunately, there's a lot of racism here in America.

S, E, V, I lived in Italy for 11 years, my son was born in Frascati, we came to America because my family is here from Cuba and for work reasons. But I must tell you that I have never seen a priest dishonor the Catholic religion so openly.

My son is a good child of good family, his father is a musician, a professional who has made 28 films in Italy as an arranger and conductor and continues to make a career in the world of music, now he has his own orchestra. By December, he will perform a piano concerto with the Miami Symphony Orchestra. As you can see, we're not street people. I am a mother who wants to raise her son in the Catholic religion, but the example of this reverend doubts in his head like a 10-year-old boy. And if he thinks so about the church there will be no religious future for him and that upsets me. Unless if Jean Paul sees a fair action on your part.

I rely on your discretion and kindness so that my name is not mentioned to Father Ted; it's strictly confidential. You and me, you have my address and my name for a possible answer.

We kiss your hands.

Kind regards.

October 10th, 1977

After I wrote the letter, I felt better, as if Avess made a confession without going to church: things still improved even compared to the neighbors. Christmas passed and by the beginning of the new year we moved back to Hialeah, on 16th Street, almost behind the Westland Mall, very close to John and Irma. This time, because of his work, Robert did not move with us

There was a neighbor from Pakistan who was a lawyer, his name was Shamir Mirsa and he was dealing with divorces, by the way. He had recently brought his wife with his two daughters and a son to the United States to live with him. The woman was very tall, with cinnamon skin and very smooth black hair, particularly long that touched her hips and still dressed like the women of Pakistan.

It was known when he was washing clothes, because he made them boil with soap leaving a nauseating smell or, and it was the same when cooking, cauliflower cabbage and broccoli. Despite closing the glass door, he gave on the park, the unpleasant smell caught the nose of anyone in those surroundings, with such force that one could not help but plug his nose.

However, they were very nice people, respectful and became our friends. At the end of the year, my brother Giovanni asked me if he wanted me to go with them to a charity dance in a city in the province of the East. We all accepted, even the couple from Pakistan.

And the day of the dance came; we went, danced, drank and ate traditional New Year grapes while having fun until the early hours of the morning.

Robert had moved in with the singer of the orchestra he had formed, and that year for Christmas he went to Maryland with his friend, to spend the end-of-year party over there. Then on his return, about the divorce he asked me if he knew or any lawyer and immediately it occurred to me my Pakistani neighbor to whom I had already mentioned and to whom Robert would pay the cost of the divorce at will.

For my part I was tired of going to her to ask for help that they denied me because she was still married, that's why the lawyer advised me to divorce as soon as possible and for the month in prile. And one morning with Kenneth and the lawyer, we went to the Miami court house to see a judge and end the marriage.

The judge asked me where Robert was, and I replied, in Shamir's place, clarifying that my husband was out of town, and continues to say:

"We ask you, Judge, to grant us a divorce, and three years have already passed since the separation. It was hard for me to be married without getting help for my kids."

The judge replied:

"I'm going to say here that if you want to reopen the case, you can do it because Mr. Robert didn't show up and those kids need medical insurance and a lot of other things."

After the judge wrote the note, I assured myself that I had been lucky. Shamir said to me:

"I think you came out of it well! The judge was good to you."

I did not wish to enter into a pointless conversation with the lawyer because I would insult him; what had I paid him for? His had only been an act of presence, in case he did not have the legal separation documents of the other lawyer to whom Avevor declared everything that had led to the failure of my marriage and what I had or lost, including my career.

Shamir did not open his mouth to ask the judge to support me. And that's the least he should have done! Ora, even without Shamir's input I could at least have more help raising my children.

With the help of my sister-in-law, who gave me all the information on where to go to be helped for rent I went to Hialeah 12th street where they were some apartments called Villa Vivian for low-income people. But I was surprised that the waiting list was a year and I couldn't wait that long.

I was disturbed that Robert knew I needed a car, that the court had ordered or to give me and what he bought were $300 cars that left me on the ground, where less mand waiting for him or, and Robert bought me an altror scrap that we threw away. That way we went looking for three cars while driving the Corvette of the year my children were left on the street.

I went to two other places and it was the same; always a waiting list, until a woman who worked in my industry told me that in Carol City, on 183 street and 47 avenues, they had low-income apartments. I didn't wait for anything; I took the address and went there.

When I arrived at the office of the aforementioned apartments, a woman took care of me very well. After holding my hand and saying smiling, "My name is Gloria."

I looked around and had already passed the first room, which was the entrance where there were some black iron chairs, a bottle of fresh water and also a shelf with office documents, illuminated by the warm sunlight coming in through the window. In the room I was in at the time, behind the door another wooden shelf was fixture on the wall and in front there were two chairs that, in turn, were in front of the desk near the window and that are when I realized that the windows had iron bars. I thought:

"It's going to be safe, since we're on the first floor."

Gloria interrupted my thoughts by telling me that she would solve my problem, asking me how much she earned or how many were the members of her family. The dissi that was my two sons and I were. I'm not going to go on living with Kenneth. So, I immediately signed the documents, taking a two-bedroom apartment, dining room, kitchen, and bathroom, and paying just $118 a month with electricity included in the price as well.

I left very happy and didn't even think about the people who lived there and who in a corner of the park, under a tree, were drinking beer. A week is expected to move to Carol City at 4601 NW 183 streets, at A11. Andra the month of June '78. The apartment had to be painted and the lock had to be dutifully changed.

I was working in an industry called in Rugi and after moving, in August I moved to another sector closer to the house named Elton Apparel Inc. the owner was a plump, bald, medium-height man who was 80 years old, but he was still strong enough to come to his business very early in the morning from Miami Beach where he lived. I was taking the bus that left me at the same door in the industry, because at the last scrap Robert had given me, the previous owner who wasn't a good person, he added sugar to the gas tank, and I didn't want to know anything about that car that would leave me on the ground.

I had recommended a retired lady who lived in those same apartments in building D named Rogelia to take care of Michelle that I accompanied in the morning and resumed in the afternoon. Rogelia prepared potatoes and rice mash with the milk that the little girl liked very much and also taught her to speak Spanish well because, with Kenneth, she spoke English and had adapted to that language.

I got along very well with Rogelia. The old woman was very religious; at home she always read the Bible and went to church every Sunday. Often religious women like her came in a car to recite prayers, two to three times a week. Despite her old age, she was very active and many times sewed clothes in her industrial machine that her son had bought her. I remember once bringing her a blue fabric with white lace to make a dress for Michelle that she sewed perfectly. We were very happy with each other's friendship.

I realized, after I moved, of the difficulties I was going to face... Living on the second floor I had to cross the stairs to get out or enter the building. There was no elevator and coming down and I could see guys selling or smoking marijuana and, to pass, I had to ask permission by carrying the baby in my arms. Later I heard from Rogelia that there was a fourteen-year-old girl who was already about to give birth to her second child, and that in building D they had killed a teacher, for drugs and other things that I did not like at all. I thought of my son Jean Paul who, being already growing up, had more freedom and could ruin his self in that environment.

So, as school was about to begin, I wanted the best for my son, like any mother who takes care of their children. And what could be better than a good education. For these reasons I called Robert and, that weekend, when he came to pick up Jean Paul, do not wait and immediately proposed to him the idea of putting Jean Paul in a ward school, although at a lot of expense, in which I would participate. To my surprise, Robert said yes and didn't need her to pay anything, that he would take care to find the school.

A few days later, Robert called me on the phone and said,

"On Saturday, we're enrolling Jean Paul at a military aviation school in Fort Lauderdale called the Florida Air Academy."

That Saturday, with Jean Paul and Robert, we went to the Ft. We handed over all the transfer data from one school to another, paid for everything that also included uniforms- without the shoes we had to buy. So, we visited the whole school, which was very big, especially the park or the stadium? Did they practice all kinds of sports?

Children who misbehaving, were punished by picking dry leaves or marching and, at the end of the week, if punished, they did not go to visit their parents in their respective homes, instead they stayed to work in the kitchen peeling potatoes and onions or washing of elle lenzuola. The first time they entered the school they had to go through a three-week period without going home- and so it was for Jean Paul.

That day was memorable for me because that school represented my son's educational future, and even when I was working, I could rest easy because sapevor that my two children were in good hands.

&&&

It was August, the hurricane season in Miami; some dissolve and others leave us wind gusts with rain. On those bad days I walked through the corridors under the buildings until I reached Rogelia's house.

After leaving Michelle, I was going to pick up the bus, but a gust of wind and rain arrived that essentially wet my head, because Avevor acape. When I got to work, Joe, the owner of the industry seeing me wet and asked me:

"But you don't have a car?"

"It's a long story. I take the bus every day to come to work!"

"Look, come with me, I've got a Ford Pinto car over there that belonged to my son, if you like; I'm going to sell it! and how much?"

"Joe, as was typical of him, put his hand to his head and said: -- Give me a hundred dollars."

"I couldn't believe it and I really thought he was sorry to see me wet like a chicken!"

"And the engines are working?"

"I start it every day because my son doesn't live here, he's in New York, and if you want you can try it.

I set the car in motion and saw that it had no defects and left. When I got out of the car I smiled and I died the hand to Joe who got lost in his because it was grande and big, and the deal was done.

On weekends, by car I would go to Ft. Lauderdale to my son and we would stay in the park for a picnic and spend the whole day. I could have eaten by bike or in the motels we rented. Anche Kenneth played ball with Jean Paul and I went either in the park with Michelle and she rolled in the grass up. Dopo years remembered or even those happy moments that would never come back.

That's how the Christmas parties came and Jean Paul spent a week on vacation at home. I cooked a turkey and only had lunch in four because my family was afraid to come where I lived, or at least that was the excuse. For the New Year Robert took Jean Paul to the club where he played with the band and I asked Rogelia to take care of Michelle so that she could go and celebrate the New Year with Kenneth in a restaurant that, with the price of her dinner, also offered everything that was used to celebrate the end of the year.

The New Year brought luck to Robert who was making arrangements for television commercials for records and Disney World. That's what he told me when he came to pick up the kids, as if he meant:

"Look if you were with me now you shouldn't live here."

In May it was Mother's Day also in the Academy. They attended with me, Kenneth and Michelle. They had prepared a chair for their parents to see the tribute the boys would offer their mothers by passing with the band playing and waving as they passed in front of high school. So, each cadet gave a white flower to their own madre. When it was Jean Paul's turn for me the camera was ready to portray a nice memory.

Returning to the apartments where she lived or once she was staying or to pay gloria rent, she asked me if I wanted to work there, that she was very busy in another place where she worked and earned more money and that's why she wanted to leave, and then added:

"I told you I was lee! I still need someone to replace me."

I thought then, "Why not, I'm right here and I don't even have to spend money on petrol to go to work!"

Wait till the week ends with the other job. And I told Gloria, I am with you!

And so, I did. Joe, the old man, was very sorry that I left because I spoke or English and understood me.

He had also taught me all or all about sewing machines, and I only took an average of800 a day, obviously he didn't want me to leave.

Well, I started working in the offices, collecting rents and answering phones for repair orders for the 150 apartments that were there. After Gloria introduced me to Bob Okuyagu, the neighbor who worked there, and gave me some explanations, about the work I had to do, disappear, and I didn't see her anymore.

Bob was very polite and well, he came from Nigeria and studied at university, he was of medium height and lean, about 28 to 30 years old.

There, we both learned a lot from the people who lived in the apartments. Remember or that there was a young man who didn't pay the rent, and we put a notice on the door for him to move. When the young man realized that he had to evacuate the apartment he became fierce and when he arrived, he was surprised that it was I who would receive it. In the back offices, Bob was in one and in the other came the administrator of Thornston Inc., the company that took care of those buildings.

With so much luck that day the administrator was there, even though it wasn't his job to deal with complaints. The young man entered, banging the door backwards, which hit the wall and did not stop until the office door where ero. Looking up, I asked him "What can I do for you?"

"You can't help me! Where's Gloria?"

And he screamed as if he had become a dog. At that point the administrator's patience ended, seeing that the man had stopped at the door and said "What are you looking for here? Can't you hear the lady talking to you? Or are you rude enough not to respect women?"

The young man became much more enraged and began to hit the walls like a tiger in the cage. Bob leaned out the door, and the maintenance man came and asked Bella:

"What's going on here?"

He made a gesture with the hand he expected and the administrator, with a sheet came out from behind his desk nimble as a panther; yet it weighed about 240 pounds. And he was over 6 feet 3 inches tall and was pushing the man out of the office saying, "Now get out of here!"

And the other "I want to talk to Gloria. Why does a Latina have to be aware of our problems? She's not of our race! It won't end like this, you'll see, you'll see!"

The administrator had already passed my office, opened the front door with one hand and held the man with the other. Behind the young man was the maintainer and they both put out the wretched, while I still kept complaining about the office and everyone who worked there?

Everyone who was present apologized for the man's misconduct and tried to comfort me because I was really nervous. Then a family man came in to pay the rent and heard him say he wasn't or their race, and then he added looking me in the face:

"We're the majority here. If a woman who doesn't belong to our race is here, I take care of our business, I'll do something too!"

So, I went to the administrator who was actually my boss and I asked him, "Or what's going to happen?"

And the boss who was already a little calmer I answer if, "Look, I will teach you to use **the pope (the computer?)** so that you realize that Gloria was the cause of all this."

Then he went to his office and took some documents from the file, showing me that of the 150 apartments had to be rented, 50 to whites, 50 to Latinos and 50 to African-Americans, and Gloria hadn't done so while living 10 families of the white razz and one of them was the detective who looked after the Anglo-American buildings. I started being afraid to work there, so he told Bob to come and go together from that day. I knew how to make a difference between tenants because I had started looking at payment cards, discovering that Gloria had accepted partial rent payments. That's why the young man we had the problem with was screaming so much that he wanted to talk to Gloria.

I was also thinking about who greeted me and who didn't. I once remember having forgotten the lights in my car were on and the men drinking under the tree in a corner of the park had noticed it and went one of them knocking on my door to get the lights off. I was very grateful and since then when they greeted me, I was responding to the greeting as well as to the lady who lived on the left side and also the other who was directly under my apartment who had a daughter about Michelle's age. Land girls played together in the evening without any problems.

A week after that incident they had to call the police with a judge's order, to forcibly remove the young man who had rebelled. While they were taking the furniture out, they discovered some bags containing drugs and arrested him. The next month, you don't know how or when they had a meeting and you gathered the signatures to get me out of the office. The boss didn't want me to leave; he said it was discrimination, and he knew it or even I, but I didn't feel calmer there and so he told the boss:

"Thank you for defending me, but I can't stay here."

The next Sunday I bought the paper to get a new job. Open the work page and right there, in front of my eyes, there was an advertisement for the Miami News separated by the Miami Herald. It only needed a few hours in the afternoon. Take your phone and call them to know the address where you should or go to ask the question.

When I arrived, I found a man of short stature well dressed, with a nice tie, very elegant and these, after having me fill out the question, told me that they would call me. I was happy, because the work was outdoors distributing newspapers and earning the same as me with old Joe when I worked 8 hours and instead- with the Miami News- I worked half and didn't have my head breathing around my neck. In addition, I could have used my time.

I started the new job using the morning, after leaving the kids at school. Anche Santiago, the skinny little man I met the day I went to do the app, was very friendly to me and gave me advice when he knew I had worked in cinema in Italy and volevor resume his career. So, he had me take some new pictures pandr get at he ate ragent to represent me contacting one three: Glen Kennedy, JV Paskoa and Marbella who were American companies. But I had my accent when I spoke or in English, and the parts were limited, so I lost my enthusiasm and didn't go to the prove. Instead, I miss at Jackson Byron's computer, remembering the lessons I took or took when he was in New Jersey. I worked until 1:00 a.m. when I arrived at Rogelia's house to pick up Michelle. That night I fell asleep and I slept with me. Dwhen Mi er or separated from Kenneth, eror alone, but apparently, I was happy and everything was fine

Jean Paul

I had asked Robert for help, but he had turned his back on me; which hurt me a lot because the children were his children. One day he told me he was going to buy a house, because the money was coming and he and his singer had bought a house at 6288 Hallandale Drive, east of Boca Raton. Soon after moving into the new home, he decided that, Jean Paul could well go to a public school because paying that large sum of money to a military school, in his opinion, was throwing money away unnecessarily. Robert didn't say to Bella that he was waiting for the school year to end up dropping the bomb. For him, payment was more important than keeping his son out of that environment and giving him a good education. Yet Robert had witnessed a violent attack by an old African-American man who had wounded a boy only because he was drunk - he was sitting in his truck and didn't want to get off.

For this reason, too, Jean Paul, at the end of the year, left military school and inserted him in the Catholic school of St. Vincent de Paul, where he did not do very well, having problems with the priests, who called me otherwise they would throw him out. And so it happened that I enrolled him in the lake Stevens junior high public school.

Every day I took him to school with his sister who had already started pre-elementary that year but Jean Paul, after a few days of school, had run away from the back door, with a small group of classmates' using lunch money to catch the bus and go to the beach. L didn't tell me at school that my son was sneaking out the back gate every morning. On the day that I had finished distributing the newspapers in advance, as I approached the entrance to the building, I saw Jean Paul get off the bus and try to hide because he had vista. At home he interrogates him discovering that he had been to the beach. The next day I drove him to the school offices where they told me that for three weeks, he had missed school. So, he had to repeat the second grade. I was very angry; there were so many things to do and so many questions I was asking about Jean Paul who decided to take him to a psychiatrist: Dr. Roger Roussero, of Jackson Memorial Hospital at the Child Adolescent Clinic. The doctor told me that the boy needed his father, but Robert didn't even want to pay or contribute to the doctor's bill and didn't care to keep his word when he said he'd come to see and the children and instead he didn't come. Jean Paul, sadly disappointed, stood dressed waiting.

So, I had to quit my job at night to look after the children Robert neglected. One day I had gone to the park to pick up, the car and it was not where the Avevor parked it. I went to see if Rogelia knew or had seen anything, as she cooks many times near the oven and if she knew what had happened to my car. I was disappointed to tell Rogelia that I had to report the incident to the police. But when I was walking through the parking lot, I looked down the street and Jean Paul arrived driving my car.

The boy could hardly be seen; he had a fisherman's hat and was so small that he sank in the seat. His friends even younger ones were sitting behind him with the conclusion that he interrupted the transmission to the machine. He had changed gears, and the bad thing is that the car was automatic.

Now I was worried about how I was going to work to deliver the papers! I called my boss Santiago, who said,

"Don't worry, you're going to get my car tomorrow, and I don't think it's worth adjusting and yours. Why don't we go see and one in the agency?"

I didn't know what to say, but I needed a car to work and that's how I would have a car thanks to Santiago who had signed up for me to buy the car and get credit at the same time. Santiago had been good to me because he really liked me. Sapevor yet that he was married and I refused him every time he complimented me. Having grown up and studied in the Catholic school and then very religious; he went to church every Sunday and every time he passed by a church he went to pray, no matter what time he was. Qi'm ttutive of his emotions.

Willie

One day in December, three days before my birthday, the car was damaged by me and Kenneth, who often phoned to find out how stessi, asked me what was wrong with the car, and introduced me to Willie Ross who was a good mechanic and proved it by repairing the car. Kenneth told him it was my birthday that week, and when he arrived that day, we went to eat at Benni Hanna restaurant in Miami Beach. After that day we heard each other on the phone and saw almost every day. Willie's intentions were to get married, but they were for his convenience, as he later realizes to the gods, but then it became too late to pull me back. Every time we saw each other he would say to me:

I think for your kids and mine, we should get married. Then he once added, "No, I care how you want to live; everything you do will be fine."

We went out with my kids, Jean Paul and Michelle, and Tania her daughter on weekends; a very nervous girl who suffered from chronic sinusitis that you didn't know when she had a cold or when she didn't, leaving Kleenex everywhere. When her father took her with him, we went together where he worked for car racing. I don't find it very funny, breathing those toxins from the cars that warmed the engines, not to mention the sord noise or when they started running while in the meantime being bitten by mosquitoes.

And he came on December 24th and I got all the gifts from my kids and his family under the Christmas tree, Call the Willies to tell him not to come because he was going to my sister Catalina's house, to Boca Raton where I was going to spend Christmas eve, and I'd greet him. The trip was about an hour's drive north. When I was already approaching Turnpike exit 28, I heard that a tire had punctured. Check the car until it stopped but I couldn't control the panic when I looked around and the trees looked like sinister figures in the dark of the night.

I was trying to control myself so as not to scare the children, but I certainly thought I wouldn't go out into those shadows of the night. I took security to the doors and thought it was important that the tire didn't get damaged. It does not rhyme there and continues to walk with the machine very slowly to do less damage to the wheel. So, he got to the exit, and before I paid the toll, I saw the phones. The skies opened and first he called my sister to pick me up and then Willie because he knew or worked on the wreckage of Miami racing cars and had a mechanical garage, and he could have the tires.

At the end of the call and after giving him an explanation of what had happened, I gave him my sister's phone number. Willie replied:

"I'm going to move right away so I can find the tires right away."

Catalina came looking for me and, at her house; with the children I had fun, eating and drinking. We also exchanged Christmas presents and remembered the distant times in Cuba that had brought me a well lontan life to from Miami where I lived or, among all those crimes. And in fact, among those delinquents there were those who, on that night, while I enjoyed or, were looting the house and the gifts of the boys. Most of the gifts had been made or taken and the others they had left were discarded, as if they had chosen. In the room they had opened some boxes of papers and photographs that had been emptied on the floor, the chaos was indescribable. They had taken Paul's Braccialetto with his name but also a German camera and some jewelry that Avevor bought in New Jersey.

It was the second time I had been visited by thieves. While all this was happening, Willie had already found two tires from a race car that his boss had lent him. When Willie arrived at the exit, he immediately recognized the car and called me on the phone. For my part, I did not feci wait, salutai the family and Catalina, with the car, took me to Willie who had almost finished changing the tires.

Willie accompanied me and the children to the apartment, and when she went to open the door, putting the key in the lock, she opened herself, revealing the disaster that the thieves had done.

The little girl saw the broken Christmas parcels and believed Santa had arrived and wanted to enter. I thought someone was still inside; Willie came in and told me I was waiting outside:

"There's no one here, we're going to call the police to report what happened."

I later discovered, from the police report, that it was the work of young delinquents, and a boy who lived with his mother in the adjacent apartment also confirmed this. He also warned where they had thrown what they had refused-on abandoned land- across the main street in front of the building, but by now I wasn't interested in looking.

That night, after giving an explanation to the children about what had happened, and that they would not have what they had asked Santa, I put them to bed and to make the door safe, I put a chair in contrast. In bed you start to consider our situation in those apartments. But now that Jean Paul was no longer at the Florida Air Academy military school, he was exposed to the corruption and crime that existed there. Men sold and bought marijuana and cocaine on the stairs leading to the second floor where MO lived and I passed by. I could see guns on my pants legs when it was hot or under my jacket in winter.

They partly respected me because they knew me, but I was asked: - How long? Think of me or my family. My brother wouldn't come to see me unless it was one of the children's birthday and by invitation, because he didn't want to bring his two daughters and his wife. My sister I considered as a mother didn't even visit me. That theft was the last thing I could stand there.

I had to move, have to do it for my children and for myself, and the only opportunity was presented by Willie. With those thoughts I fall asleep. The next day that was the Christmas party sapev, or already being invited by Willie to meet his family.

Willie's mother bought gifts for my children for whom I was very grateful. It didn't take more than two weeks and Willie gave me a diamond ring to seal the engagement. Her mother took care of the wedding and all expenses, while the stag party was organized by her sister, a 220-pound woman, without manners and with the voice like that of a man. She had been a teacher of physical education and now worked as an assistant to a principal; she had been married and divorced twice.

The mother was the exact opposite of her daughter, highly refined and involved in the greater benefits of the state of Florida and was preparing to retire as vice president of a well-known bank in Florida, where she had worked for more than 30 years.

It was all happening so fast that I didn't have time to think... One day as we went for a walk with the boys, Willie was driving and I was sitting next to him. The conversation was about marriage but it was as if he had inadvertently said what … he thought aloud:

"Now I'm going to be the one to sincere. And if I get married, they can't deny me custody of you Tania."

After I realized the meaning of those words, when we came back from the cinema, the same day, in the apartment park there was an argument between me and Willie because of his daughter. Volevor give him back the ring saying the wedding wouldn't go well. He stood in position like the swordsmen, his paralyzed arm curled up on my chest and his left that pointed in my direction and said:

"You give it to my mother and you tell him you don't want to get married."

What answer, devoid of logic was that? Stavor to marry his mother? I was surprised, but I didn't think it was because he was sick. Nothing had made me realize that, like me, many other people did not know him. If I had read Willie's divorce papers with his first wife, I wouldn't have married him.

He had a criminal record. He had, in fact, kidnapped the four-year-old girl for eight months, after raping and beating his wife. He also suffered from seizures, taking phenobarbital and dilantil to control him. Non sapevor how to behave with a mind-ill person, who did not want to recognize him, but I had seen something strange in him.

Once he had come at night to see me and d had stayed at the door, without entering, with the twisted figure he had from quando he had been born (one leg, the right was shorter than the other, the foot was smaller than the other and the right arm had paralysis. Gsmiles at them and invites them once again. Willie with his arms crossed and leaning on his longer leg, tried to straighten himself by touching a height of 6 feet 2.5 inches, then smiled so well that his blue right eye changed color and then opened it with a grimace of the lower facial muscles.

Kenneth had introduced me to his childhood friend, Willie, telling me that he had worked for 9 years in Miami-Dade schools and only thinking about my children and the situation I was in or, in less than two months, I had or married a man.

A week before the wedding, Willie's aunt rented their house with an option to buy it. None was far from Ellen's house, 5 blocks away.

As concerns about the marriage were disappearing, Ellen invited me to spend that week at her house, so that he could move me into the new house and repair, meanwhile some holes in the wall of Jean Paul's room that he believed or he had done with a mace, instead I knew, later, by Jean Paul himself who had punched them when he was frustrated because his father had left him waiting after telling him that he was looking for him or that he was hurting at school and disobeyed me by venting resentment in that way.

And it came on the day of the wedding, February 14, 1982. She was accompanied to the altar by my brother John, while Willie's eldest daughter, Tatiana, was a bridesmaid and Willie's mother's cousin witnessed it. Michelle and Tania were the flower ladies chosen by Kayla and Zoraida's another daughter. Jean Paul, after putting the flowers on the lapel, came to the altar because he had the rings.

After the ceremony there was a reception at Ellen's house, where I met Martha's invited friends who were school principals and teachers, and Ellen's guests were authorities of the Salvation Army, the Moose Club, where she had been elected Florida state ruler that year.

I will remember that year in 1982- when I saw you on 38th Street in Hialeah- as the most unfortunate or terrifying, of my life. Tania, her daughter Willie, when she came on weekends proved possessive and causing problems between us. Willie always spoke ill of his mother, sowing hatred towards her.

The girl, by the way, one day went to Jean Paul's room and began to take what was not his and when Jean Paul returned, he realized something was missing and there were broken things, he went to Tania's room and broke a poster he had on the wall. When he then complained to Willie, he came to Jean Paul and seemed to want to eat him alive and - without finding out and first the truth slapped him.

So, I went to defend my son. Land things got worse, while between screams and pushes they pulled out each other's dirty rags. I slept in the room with the little girl. The next day the kids went to school, so I was alone with Willie and I was getting ready to go to work and, when I was already on the front door, Willie was standing in front of me blocking the exit. I wanted to argue and tried to get to the other door but Willie running could block the one I was trying to open as well but his longer legs made sure he got there before me.

The situation was over and the situation was over. We fought and threw him at a reclining chair that bounced hitting his head. I pulled out all my strength because there was no one who could help me and pushed him with a kick while he got up staggering. Cors then turned to the phone but he hung up, he continues to run to the back door but he can't even open it to because I'm prevented from doing it. Luckily, I heard the phone ringing. I ran fast, I pressed him and finally shouted at "Help, police!"

Willie picked up the phone while running to a window trying to open it to and at the same time asking for help. The person at the other end of the phone was my boss of the job who called the police. When they arrived, they knocked on the door and knocked harder and louder; it opend and threw me out but asked them not to leave until they got clothes for me and my children, which was when I was already in the car, Willie grabbed a door and didn't let me go. I then asked the cops to speed up and the car left fast.

So, I went to school to pick up the kids, so I didn't think much about what had just happened, but I realized it wasn't over. Willie had followed me there and I realized that he was so close to the car that he could see through the rearview mirror, the Ford truck he was driving.

When I accelerated, he did too, and when I reached as top on a big street, Willie made his mark with the lights. I was scared for the children and I didn't stop. He swerved to the right approaching our car while he had to pull me further to the right by climbing onto the sidewalk so I wouldn't crash.

The little girl was crying and screaming as Jean Paul said to me: -Run! Speed up, faster! Stronger! -

I was able to straighten the car, going back to the stop on the big road. I was hoping someone who lived in those houses could see and call the police.

I was back at the stop when, Willie manode and put the truck almost in front of my car, forcing me to stopi.

Immediately got out of the truck, ran to my car, reached the window taking the keys and got into the truck and left. The children and I were puzzled. I thought "What do we do now?"

I knew that police cars often passed through these big streets and after only five minutes one stopped. That's how I recounted what had happened and while I was talking, Willie came back, and the policeman forced him to give me the keys and stayed there until I left and finally got to the hotel I had contacted.

A week later, with the help of my boss, we started looking for a house and found it, moving in immediately. Willie had calmed down or, and had called me to work because he wanted to come back to me, but I didn't want to hear about him anymore, and he went to work, while the police officer brought me the papers prepared by the divorce attorney.

Jean Paul had taken a datsun truck to Willie who had become angry and wanted to go back to life, just because of the truck, with me leaving him because I knew it wouldn't last. For a week Jean Paul had left school during the day and had studied at night but with little result while preparing the necessary documents to insert him into the Job Corps.

When Robert learned that Willie had taken the truck back from Jean Paul, he said:

"I have a Chevrolet, Chevette, for you, if Willie fixes it."

Willie, to do me what I liked to and bring me back to him, said yes. Jean Paul left for the Job Corps in North Carolina.

There, all the young people were African-American. Because he had been threatened with death, even for a game of billiards, He complained to a superior and he said:

"Here, every man must think of himself!" Jean Paul did not let himself be knocked down but they were trapper for him.

That day he hid in the mountains, walking all day hungry and thirsty, until a *guajiro,* in a truck, picked him up and took him to the bus station where he called me to send him the ticket to Miami.

Robert, meanwhile, wanted to take back the Chevette he had given Jean Paul and came to pick him up, without paying for the job for the clutch, and took it away from him, giving it to his wife's sister. Having filed for divorce Willie, he asked his mother for a few thousand pains and bought a house for him and me. Robert was taking an interest in his daughter, with the excuse that Michelle would take care of Sharon, the daughter she had with his new wife, and I took her home on weekends.

I didn't see anything wrong with that, but I thought:

"Sharon's feelings seem to have softened with the baby!"

When she left, Michelle was 9 years old and was starting to develop so much that you could see the tips of her breasts through her clothes. I bought the adjustment devices for the girls and I was happy for her.

One day Robert took her *barefoot and without regiseni.* He doesn't think of anything wrong, and Robert promised that he wouldn't do it again, but that it was very hot and why make so many clothes wear? I didn't imagine for a moment that the man I trusted, in giving him my daughter- our daughter, on weekends - was sexually abusing the girl! Who would have guessed? He was the father!

Going back to Jean Paul, in those two years there was so much resentment towards his father that he had not taken care of him, and Willie had never accepted it, so the boy left the house and did not want to eat at the table with us because Willie chose just meal time to fight. So, he's looking for friends in places he shouldn't have had and with people who had nothing to offer, like a certain Byron who lived on a cow and pig farm. Well, with that guy they took a 50-pound pig from the farm, and put it in the back seat of the car. When they grabbed him by the ears, to get him out of the seat the pig got scared and the excrement came out, thus dirtying the car.

Once again with David Pinchar they took the aluminum doors and windows that served to protect the house from the fury of difficult times, such as hurricanes, tornadoes, etc... That's why he didn't have a

Butt at and away, and he still took a sewing machine and when I realized the things were missing, he gave the money back to the person he had just sold it to and bring the items back.

Another day he sold an empty box of tools from 1954, full of rust for how old he was, but he was with the Willies and his father had given it to him. Willie, he didn't think much about it, went looking for him and found him at the supermarket and called the police, claimed that the box cost$2000.00 just to stain Jean Paul's criminal record because the hatred was mutual.

The police took Jean Paul, hand cuffed him and, only after three days, released him under my responsibility, but he should have been home when the officer came to see him by surprise and did not find him. They arrested him again for 14 days. Eror furious with Willie, since he can't do anything to him, threatens him with divorce if he doesn't tell the judge the truth and he did.

To get back in the car in Miami I drove until tired, thus gaining time and in 5 days we returned.

When I got to Miami Also, I had a problem to solve with Robert who didn't want to send me the boys' money, so I had, while Michelle was present, a heated conversation with him on the phone telling him: "OK, I will send you the baby so that you can raise it; this way you will find out how much it costs to support the kids."

Michelle then began to cry and after hanging up, she asked her:

"What's wrong? I thought you liked playing with your little sister."

Then the little girl told me that her father had kissed her on the mouth and touched her breasts; he was asleep and he had lay on the bed with her, etc. and cc.

I couldn't call the Miami Lakes police, but it had to be where the event occurred. The degenerate Robert lived in Ft. Lauderdale and there I met Detective Barth who investigated the case and sent Michelle to the Jackson Memorial rape center. Michelle told Det. Barth, where, when and how the facts were going and what his father had told him. And Michelle repeated Robert's words:

"Do you have to learn these things for when you grow up! This is our little secret and I'm going to buy you a Cabbaga Patch doll and even for when you turn 16, I will give you a Corvette."

Not only was he stealing his body but also his mind, and his innocence. Volevor kill him. Eror been a peaceful person all his life but it was too much! Every time I saw him in one of the many stools, in court, I wanted to tear him to pieces and throw it at crocodiles, or take a gun and empty the ela in his head, but they wouldn't let the guns pass in court. Among other things, Robert's bastard, to defend himself, claimed that the degenerate had been Michelle's brother: Jean Paul.

The little girl, with tears streaming down her cheeks, told the Det. Barth and the district attorney, a Niel Dupriest, who was his father the one they had to arrest and who was very sorry for Sharon, her little sister, thinking about the things she was going to face growing up with Robert.

I called the lawyer and asked him, "Why don't they arrest him yet?"

What did you expect? Waiting to call Janet Reno, who was a Florida prosecutor at the time, they gave the detective an arrest warrant. After the arrest, the woman called me, because in her mind Robert was innocent, but I made the facts clear to her. Robert hired a good criminal lawyer who cost him, they say, $8000. After that they took his passport away so he could not go to France and also prevented him from contacting the child until he was 18 years old. He could not work anything other than in West Palm Beach, F. Lauderdale or Miami, awaiting trial.

In January 1985 Jean Paul started working in a hardware store called Baron Hardware and bought a Kawasaki 650 motorcycle, which one night while everyone in the house slept, was stolen from him, under the window of his room. The next day I went with him to the corner garage to get gas, and we met a guy who lived in the house in front of us. The boy, without delay told us that he knew where the bike had been taken. A few months later, one night when I was alone with Michelle, we heard gunshots toward the neighbors' house and the dog started barking.

Peering out one of the windows we noticed that the police special weapons team (SWAT) had surrounded the house and when they gave the signal, they forced to open the door and arrested everyone who was there, and also one who wanted to escape from the back and who they captured in the same yard.

I saw a policeman or who had taken off his jacket and was wrapping it around his arm, waiting for the attack of the dog who wanted to jump the fence, I went out shouting the dog's name "JR! Jr!"

By this name, Junior had been named, in honor of the owner... and he was as bad as he was. After that incident, JR had murderous instincts and jumped the fence into his neighbors' house, killing the cats and dragging them in his mouth, depositing them in front of the door so he could see what he had done. And Willie had to get rid of dead cats, then he started killing chickens that had neighbors, eating them with bones, leaving only the feathers that stuck to his mouth with blood.

Problems with JR increased when he began biting children walking down the street in front of the house: the dog believed that all this was his territory and that no one or nothing could invade him. But Willie and I also had other ideas as we were trying to darlor anyone who wanted it... Well, thank God, Jean Paul's friend who owned a farm wanted it. So, they took him to the truck and that was the end of JR because, on the farm, he started biting the cows too and had to put him to sleep in an eternal dream. A few months after JR's death, my boss gave me a 4-month-old Cocker Spaniel puppy that was one of the most beautiful, with long ears and reddish hair. He was very smart but Willie wanted the dog to lie on the bed with him and on the living room sofa giving bad habits to the dog and I didn't like this.

Rusty, so the boys called the dog but Willie sent them away, and took him out. I bought him food, but the dog belonged to him without anyone giving it to him.

Willie had a former brother-in-law, Buzzart who was a mechanic and friend of his family. A berry was behind the house repairing a car and Jean Paul, Mark, Rick and Mike were playing and recording the music. After playing, for at least an hour, and with a cassette already recorded, they went out to cool off and rusty also went out with them.

From the street, two African-Americans rushed in; They had a fight and one had a gun in his hand pointing at the other who was running and seeing Mike's car with the door open because they were listening to the tape they had just recorded, he got into the car to hide and save himself from a safe bullet.

While the boys, watching the young man come with the gun pointed at them, they fled from all sides, leaving Jean Paul alone and Rusty who began barking. The young man pointed the gun at Jean Paul who said to him "Hey you, get out of here with your troubles!"

The dog felt the danger, barking and managing to attract the attention of the unfortunate young man who pointed the gun at the dog, shooting and shooting him, saving Jean Paul.

While all this was happening, the boy who was hiding in the car, seeing that the keys were in the dashboard, turned on and left, but failed to pass 47th Street for traffic, because Mark and Mike kept him behind, reaching him in less than two blocks. Finally, the boy got out of the car taking the keys and laying them on the ground. Mike what he wanted was to get his Camaro back, that's why he let him escape.

I, who was inside the house, heard the gunshot and the voice of Jean Paul screaming:

"Rusty is injured, Willie, Mammina, Rusty è ferito,come!"

On the way out I met Buzzart who said, "I called 911, you have to take Rusty to the hospital, in Miami there is an animal hospital that is also on duty on Sundays."

I called the police and when I went out you found that Willie was kneeling talking to Rusty crying. Quella was the first time I saw him cry, he was so sarcastic and tildy that I never thought he could cry ever.

The police came, filled out the documents and went to look for the offender but they did not find him in the house. He was arrested the next morning after learning that the boy was named Randolf and had a list of crimes since he was 14 years old. In the trial he was sentenced to 3 years for shooting the dog.

Rosty saved himself by costing $1500 and staying in the hospital for three months. They put a steel bar on him to replace the bone and when he came back, I died him to Willie.

Everything was always under Willie's control that when he came home and there was no peace. He came to see what had not been done or what had been done without his permission. I couldn't change the arrangement of the furniture either.

I couldn't even spend the money of the guy's Robert sent me without his knowledge. I counted pennies while Willie always had a roll of bills in his pocket Jean Paul said:

"On the day they're going to assault him with all that money! Willie's mother said that, too."

When Christmas came, Willie told me to make a list to send the guys to buy gifts and of course the list was clothes. I would have thanked him but it was not to my taste and also for my compleanno which was in December, when his sister bought clothes and pants very often the ones, he would donate to the church gave them to me. And I was like, "I'm not going to do this.

"What a difference from when you were making movies!"

(HERE YOU CAN INSERT SCENES FROM THE MOVIES)

I was depressed and gave me not to drink but to eat. I had lost my line, and I remember that among the other insults I received Willie called me *fat* and hippopotamus. And when I wanted to eat Cuban bread or guava cake, he would say, "That's why you get fat; you're buying that shit."

So, if I had the desire for a dessert, I had to eat it secretly.

Tired, however of so much sarcasm for my weight, I bought dietary toast and frul lati

I put them in a kitchen cabinet, to pick them up for breakfast and lunch. As always Willie was aware of what Avevor bought. He had gone, that day, to the refrigerator looking for something to eat and not having found it became hysterical, and from the locker where Avevor dietetics began to take everything and throw it on the floor screaming angrily:

"Ah, your and Michelle's things remember to buy them but my ... May I be struck by lightning! - Lor I was watching and I couldn't believe he threw food on the floor and the only thing he told me was: - Well, now pick it up!"

Stopping washing the dishes I had started when Willie arrived in the kitchen, I wiped my hands and left, trying to avoid a bigger fight because I couldn't or could no longer bear to be in the presence of someone as intolerable as Willie.

So, I decided to give him the treatment of silence for three days. Another problem was watching TV. Willie and I had a TV in our room, and the guys also had one in theirs so there were no problems for the different programs we wanted to see at the same time. I didn't go to the living room to watch TV, and I would stay in the room with Willie, who would choose the programs he liked and I couldn't watch Spanish channels, so when friends asked me if I'd seen Sabado Gigante or a telenovela I was left in limbo without knowing what to say. I wasn't basically free to see or know the customs or customs in my native language.

On the evening of January 20, Willie was more nervous than usual because he had sent his work truck to the mechanic and they hadn't finished it for the appointed day. It was time for the meal. I eror standing in front of the kitchen and stavor serving food. Willie was sedutor at the table with his back turned to Michelle who was standing on the arch of the door, between the kitchen and living room, watching television. The girl sang softly; she loved the music and had studied clarinet and piano at school which she then left for the choir. On Saturdays the portavor by a singing teacher and she sang the canzonitrasmess and on TV.

I had already put the plate with food in front of Willie when throwing away the chair, with a lot of violence; he went into the living room passing by Michelle like a bullet and went to turn off the television.

Then, he stood again saying in a sarcastic and rabid tone "Ora you no longer have the music to sing with! And I also told you I don't want you to sing and I don't want to listen to that music!"

Michelle sat at the table to eat the food she had or already served her but had no fork or knife, stopped and went looking for them by sitting down again. After cutting the steak with a knife, he turned it away with a disgusted face because he had passed on his appetite.

Immediately Willie took the knife and threw it forcefully on the table to which I said:

Don't be angry, nothing serious happened. A girl has those abrupt ways, it's not like she does it on purpose! And Michelle added:

"It's in my way, (THE SONG?) what do you want me to do?"

Then Willie punched the girl in the face, telling him "You must learn to become a lady!

You're just like your brother!"

To which I intervened, "Do not compare the girl to Jean Paul, who you know are two different people!" I also knew that that discussion wouldn't end, since Willie liked to start a fight, and knowing that the food was going to cool down I said to Michelle, "Go eat in the living room …"

The girl took her plate and went to the living room to watch television and Willie got up and turned off saying, "I didn't give you any permission to watch TV.- punishing Michelle without having done anything wrong."

When I went to his room I said to my daughter, "Michelle, I know it's hard to live with him, but we have to wait a little longer. Try to stay calmat. Don't answer him, he's sick."

And Michelle, "But Mom, I can't take it anymore, take me to my Aunt Caridad's house!"

I was just about to explode with Willie and his mistreatment of the boys. What more did I have to endure for my children?

This was no longer a home to educate anyone, not even the dog Rusty... I had believed, when I was Avevor worked for the schools in Dade County, that he would be a good father to my children, but now he is convinced that it was not good at all and, before he lost the love of my children, the only thing I had left was to leave, worried especially for Michelle. I rented an apartment, a truck and I traveliito Hialeah without saying anything to Willie; the guys were happy. Christmas wa coming and Jean Paul had bought a car. In Michelle's change served as a therapy for nerves without Willie's torments. I then went to the family lawyer, paid $300 to live quietly. When Willie found out that

Avevor called the lawyer told him that I had returned with him and that he had to stop the divorce papers. The lawyer believed his lie and forked the$300 and even while we were employed in the same company for part of the job because Willie was my supervisor.

So, I was again forced to go home with Willie and his sarcasm, his manias, his *jealousy, his epilepsy attacks* and the pills and phenobarbitol and dilantin that were already starting to cause so many problems. Since I have or do not work, Willie, he sends me to the pharmacy to look for the pills for him in the right amount to last all month. But each time the pharmacist had to call the doctor to confirm whether he could give them to him or not. Having passed an anno the doctor replied no and added:

"I need to see Willie in my office! And when I told him, I'm going to get in the way of saying,

The doctor just wants my money. I've been taking those meds since I was 17, and now why does he have to go to the doctor?"

He finally called the doctor and he convinced him to take an exam and it turned out that he had cholesterol at 394, almost to the point of inflicting a collapse on him. I took advantage of a moment that was alone with the doctor to talk to him about Willie's comport chin and asked him if he didn't need a stronger medicine to control his nerves. The doctor looked at me and shaking my head, he made me:

"I'm sorry but it's the maximum dosage I can give him, from here on out and go to a psychiatrist!"

And he gave me a note with the doctor's name recommended. When he got home with the recipe, Willie took it and threw it in the trash.

When Willie felt better, with all the people who knew him, he started talking about me about my children, who couldn't live without him, that Jean Paul wasn't helpful and didn't like working, of the friends he had and that I left him, but he knew he would always comeback.

He spent hours on the phone, until the thing reached my ears through a friend. Then you surprised him even as he talked to his brother and Buzzart, so I told him that he was the least suitable to talk because, it was petty as a man to highlight those ridiculous things to people when he was still living next to the people he spoke about badly. And she had more to hide because her daughter Tania took all kinds of drugs and reminded him of when she had to get up at 3 am and go looking for the boys because they couldn't handle Tania, who had hallucinations and sawan imaginary train approaching her. And three people couldn't put it inside the auto.

Not only did she take marijuana but everything presented to her as a drug. That's why he never had any money! And I remembered all the bad times when he kicked me out by locking my son in jailor when throwing food on the floor- he was screaming. I would have liked at that moment, really to be a hippopotamus, as he called me to sit on him and crush him.

The fight was long and from that moment you start going to sleep in the living room and he would hit the door because he knew it bothered me until the wooden door broke and he touched cambiarlto with an iron ore. Her family didn't come to see me because Willie had snubbed her- soeror alone!

To Willie, to further mortify me came the idea of taking his daughter into custody, so that he could come and live with us. He told the lawyer that the family had had for many years and crucified Tania's mother, using the Human

Resources Service (HRS) to speed up the investigation, both on the mother and father.

And when they came home, I told them how they went with Willie, so they didn't give custody.

Willie had an argument with the lawyer and called him incompetent, after he sent me to look for the will and it was revealed that the lawyer had told the secretary to give her that or that was of Willie's father who is called after him and had died a few years earlier.

When Willie realized it was his father's, he read it noting that his brother, who lived in Pennsylvania, had been excluded. Instead of asking his mother that she had been so generous to him, or called his father's half-brother and sent him a copy of the will, because Willie knew that when his brother was a two-year-old, his mother died leaving him a small inheritance. And with some of that money they put him in a military school and when he came out, he told his father to invest the rest of his inheritance together by buying 5 acres of land in the gardens of Hialeah.

When Willie's brother grew up, he asked his father:

"When are you going to name the land in my name?" He repeated it several times and was heard answering:

"Don't worry, I'll worry about you at the right time!"

But by the time he died the documents had not yet been transferred to him and Willie's mother, having agreed with their two uncles, who had apart in the business and sold the land for $250,000.

THE MEANING IS NOT UNDERSTOOD: The phone calls between Willie and his brother until the latter decided to make a legal appeal to criansa's mother instructing Willie to find a lawyer and this is taken from his brother, when his mother knew, I call to count Willie and Bela went with him, took away the keys to the house

and the credit cards he had lent him saying I'm going to pretend I've already buried you, and I don't want to see you here anymore! "

So, she lost the trust of her mother and so on, and they didn't win the case, because she was married to Willie's father and under Florida law, she had erected what was her husband's. He spent some time and they called Tania's mother at the school she was going to open where she kept the books because she had a lock and they found marijuana, the girl said it wasn't hers and other stories arose (IF YOU DELETE IT, IT'S BETTER OR MAKE IT UNDERSTANDABLE)

Willie took another lawyer again, a Bruce Crown, and paid over a thousand dollars. They went back to court once again and Tania had already turned 15 and said she wanted to live with her father, Willie had custody and Tania and came to live with us... and it was for three people.

I had to take her to school and, she walked with a box of Kleenex, leaving used tissues all over the house leaving them, whereever she blew her nose. Find more even under the lunch table! It was not known when she had a cold or when she didn't have it because Tania used it when she didn't want to go to school, she told her father that she had a cold and so she stayed home watching TV.

The mother did not take care of her and when she was little, she sent her to school with 50 cents to have lunch and if the cereal was finished, she went to school without breakfast. Then if she behaved badly for some reason, he punished her. That's why I tolerated her and felt sorry for her and just as Michelle had suffered albeit differently and remembering that she had once asked me to take her to her aunt Caridad's house in Boca Raton, I had called my sister to send Michelle for a while.

And so I did, and Caridad believed that Michelle would never return to Miami and treat her like a daughter, introduced her to her friends and Michelle conebbe Mayra, a girl who had moved from New York to Florida and lived on the same block, attended the same school, and became good friends.

One afternoon Michelle was visiting Mayra and suddenly saw a man running from door to door as if he were afraid, and asked Mayra "Who is that man?"

"What man? There's no one here."

Michelle then described it, and she admitted that it was her uncle who had died, and that he was running because - before he died- he had had a strong argument with his father and -when he died-there was no talk of it and therefore sought forgiveness.

Everything was as Michelle said and she had never come to New York or met that man. When Caridad found out what had happened, he took Michelle to the home of a friend of hers who believed in spiritualism. Dopo a po' the woman took out a deck of cards that seemed used, and gave it to Michelle saying they were her aunt's. In Cuba she had given them to her,assouvenirs, so you could take them to Florida. Michelle took the cards and had never read the futuro with or without the decks of cards and said, among other things, that a boy in Cuba had problems at home with his father due to an illness he had contracted in a distant country when he went to war, and that is why they did not want him at home. The woman was amazed at how that 16-year-old girl could know all this because her nephew, the Cuban government, had sent him to Angola, Africa, and contracted the AIDS (HIV). The woman was so impressed that she gave the cards to Michelle.

Another time a friend of Caridad's named Diana went to visit her and Michelle saw a white puppy who was thirsty and told Diana "Your puppy is looking for water."

Diana, I answer if, "Non I have a dog but tell me what color itis?"

And when Michelle described it to him, the woman said,

"That puppy remembered me and died a long time ago."

I knew about Michelle's psychic powers, because when she was 4 years old, she played with virgin children and when I asked her who she was talking to, she described to them that her mother was wrapped in a yellow light and when she touched the babies who had diapers, or someone came into the room where they disappeared into the drawers. (CLARIFY THE MEANING)

As Michelle grew older, her powers grew with her, until an English teacher told her to be careful not to tell anyone because not everyone understood parapsychology and they might have thought she was crazy. Since then, little by little, he took care of people seeing in the past or in the present or the future. Things didn't go very well for her at Boca Raton. Caridad didn't want Michelle on the phone for a long time so much that he ripped her phone off the wall and tossed it against the other wall. Michelle then called me and told me what had happened. I thought:

"Sono things to ragazzi that always want to be on the phone but there was no need to throw the phone against the wall."

After a week, I called her again and the girl said to me:

"I'm not eating well because Aunt Cari doesn't cook for me."

So, I went looking for Michelle, but she didn't want to go back to living with Willie; she still remembered the bad times she had experienced, and Tania always wanted the whole room to herself. He added that he wanted to live with his brother, who had also moved out of Willie's house at the time. But they were two completely different people and they didn't even have the same friends. Call or my kids every day and Willie to conquer Michelle, as she was away from school and graduation approached, she had given him a car so he could move easily. Another car gave Tania.

Michelle filled the car with her friends and, almost every weekend, they went to the beach or the movies and even to favorite singers' concerts.

One day visiting her cousin who was organizing acrylics at the time, getting married and having two children, a boy and a girl, Michelle told her she wanted to move in and her cousin invited her to her. Willie told her that he had gone to submit an application to barnet bank from where his mother had retired after 30 years and that Michelle had a chance to be hired. That's how she started working there part-time because she hadn't graduated yet.

One morning in May, as I finished the ride, I did every morning and came home at 10:20, while parking the car, I saw a gold-colored car, of an old model, parked on the side of the house. At the time, I didn't think I was the victim of a robbery, but I thought it was someone Willie sent to fix the car, that's why I said to the black man, saying hello to him with his hand:

"Hey, what do you want! And what are you doing?" Black, confused, didn't lose his temper and replied that he was checking something here. I had never seen it, I tried to look inside the car but the windows were very dark and I couldn't see anything, nor do the young girls and Willie's gun who were already in the front seat of the car. I looked into the trunk and realized it was a robbery when I saw my stereo inside.

I stuck for a moment, thinking, OMG, what am I doing?! Those seconds alone were enough for the man to run away and get in the car and as he did, I grabbed my stereo and held it in his hands, while the man walked away insulting me and I did the same. I tried to get the registration number by realizing I had taken it off from that day when they had alerted the whole house.

The next month, Michelle graduated and because Jean Paul would come and see her sister on such a special day, I would put on a shirt and bring it to him. On the way back we stopped at the Winn Dixie supermarket to buy Pepsi Cola for Willie. When I was about to pay, in front of me, was the man who had robbed me a month earlier.

I recognized him and pretended not to know who that man of a sturdy build about a meter and a half tall was who stood in front of me; then he came out of the queue where I was and went to another checkout to, pay and left the supermarket. When I left, I saw the man driving a gas company truck with the name and logo of the badge. Back home, she tells the story to Willie who called the detective who was handling the case giving him all the details. They never took it because the man left for North Carolina.

It was three years since Tania came to live with me and her father. Willie was dominant with her and didn't give her a chance, and on the other hand she didn't like Hialeah's school without Michelle (so she said) but the reality was that she didn't even like studying and she wanted to get out of her father's clutches because she was realizing it was better to live with her mother.

Things, as always, didn't go very well with Willie, and so Michelle and Jean Paul decided to move in an apartment in Miami Lakes on their own. Only Michelle worked and things went from bad to worse, so Jean Paul worked at home with me and Willie.

They were already adults and could not go on in society because they came from a family that had never functioned as such.

Jean Paul had been abandoned by his father, since Robert had divorced me and had never been accepted by Willie. He had never made an effort to study and the friendships he was attending were among the worst. The same thing happened with Tania. The mother and father put the girl in the same position as Jean Paul, although her father said it was not the truth.

Michelle was the strongest and most determined. He went to college, graduated and began his banking career. After Jean Paul returned home, Willie charged him rent, and hired Tania in the company he worked for, but she made him look bad and they always quarreled.

One day Willie gave him A SLAP?) on his face, he charged me with waking Tania up to go to work but she only got up when she wanted and it happened that Willie came home by surprise and surprised her asleep so he invited her, "Either you prepare or leave!"

And that's what she wanted; so, he called his mother and went with her again, as Tania was 19 years old.

Now he was left with only Jean Paul in Willie to have a fight with and but Jean Paul stayed in the house when Willie wasn't home or sleeping. I remember one August afternoon, Jean Paul had to make a phone call while Willie and I were about to go out.

Willie tells Jean Paul, "Hang up this phone call!"

"Just a moment... I'm already finishing up."

"This is my house, and if I tell you to hang up, and you don't, well, I'm going to hang up!"

And he hung up the phone, to which, Jean Paul insulted him by saying that he had no education and they almost punched each other. I middled myself between the two of them and the discussion was with me then.

"Poor me, I always paid for broken dishes."

After Tania ruined Michelle's car, she asked Willie to buy another: an 8-cylinder green Mustang, which she paid with the money earned in the bank. After being in her cousin's house, Michelle came back to me, as things were not going very well between them, for some furniture taken from Michelle, for her cousin's house. They spent a year changing the furniture three times until the furniture factory grew tired and put the lawyers to withdraw them. Cousin, it didn't matter that Michelle's credit was ruined and she never paid the bill.

Michelle often went out with friends in her car and she didn't miss the guys who courted her. One day he went to Coconut Grove and met a young man named Jose Rojas; they went out, liked each other and Michelle went to live with him and his parents. After a year of living together, Bella told them to get married and they were planning it by the end of the year. Willie and I made the money for the house and the wedding was celebrated in December 1996. He was very handsome and elegant with the bridesmaids of the Protestant church. Michelle's father came with his daughter Sharon but did not take Michelle to the altar. It was Willie who paid about $8,000. He raised Michelle and had that honor.

After the reception, the couple honeymooned in North Florida with a new truck they bought at the MaroonDodge.

Now that the boys had grown up, I would go with Willie on Saturdays to work with him. One in the morning-around Hollywood, after passing under a bridge we saw three men who looked Mexican.

The fatter of them went cycling and when I saw him, I told Willie to be careful seeing how he was driving with one hand and looking around. Well, all of a sudden, he started looking back at the car that Willie and I were in, and he stood in the middle of the street. So, I got nervous yelling at Willie

"Hold on! Brakes!" But the man didn't even move by taking the path of our car. What scared me was that Willie didn't stop the car even though I was screaming. The man looked back for the last time, Willie began to advance until he bumped into the unfortunate man who fell over the bonnet of the car, rolled and fell to the ground. He wasn't hurt, but he was drunk.

Then he said to Willie, "Kill me, deliver me! (in Spanish)."

And Willie, who didn't understand, said to me, "Who knows if we want the police or an ambulance?"

And when I asked him, it looked like he hadn't heard. The other two men, while seeing their companion on the ground, said: "Or not, no need, we will take care of him, they can leave if they want."

And Willie told him we weren't going to move out of there and call the police. The two men helped the other to get up and this came up to me and said: "Questo resolves with a bullet!"

It was clear that he was drunk, his way of speaking with his tongue entangled in the liquor consumed gave him the strength to speak and I understood that the man was threatening us, so I told them

"If you don't want to call the police, get out of here! Or I call her because she's threatening us..."

At this point the men grabbed the drunk and started walking, but not before taking the bicycle which was all bent by the blow received.

Willie got in the car with me but didn't leave until the men crossed the street, then said "Look back if they get our license plate. I don't trust these people, I guess they're here illegally, so they didn't want the police to call."

Before Michelle graduated, the singer Robert had married when he divorced me had filed for divorce, and here the hand of divine power intervened to give me justice and Robert was left with nothing. The money he had in the bank and had pulled it out, a few years earlier, when he had sold the house in Boca Raton, Florida, and had the brilliant idea that it was his father saying it was for Sharon, when he would have turned 18, while my children had nothing! Well, now there he is, Robert who remained like the rooster of elmoron, without feathers and without singing.

This affected his overall state of health, to the point that one day, while he was driving, the pressure had increased, he had a dizziness losing control of the car, which collided with another and Robert broke his snout... thus losing two teeth.

Moving forward, the daughter and the work remained friends. They knew a 64-year-old man who attended the club where they played, believed he had money and join the relationship, didn't last long and got another divorced man and had a daughter Sharon didn't like, but his mother married him.

To Sharon's misfortune, it turned out that the man was drinking and arguing strongly with his mother, The little girl who was already about 14 years old defended her mother, until he got married and gave her a choice, if she didn't leave him she would have gone to Ohio with her grandparents, well, they divorced and moved in alone leaving the man in the apartment when Robert found out because he moved in with whom he didn't close very well with Sharon and changed the phone number and computer number without even giving it to Michelle. And so, he lost contact with the family. (TO BE ELIMINATED BECAUSE IT IS INCOMPREHENSIBLE AND EVEN USELESS TO THE STORY)

In August 1997 she tired of having to endure all kinds of problems and Willie as always did not want to go to the doctor for an annual check-up, in one of the many quarrels, call the police and while talking to one of the officers they explained to me the Baker Act. The next day he went to a judge to enforce that law and they took Willie for a psychological check-up for three days. When Willie was brought under control in a clinic, he started calling everyone he knew. He didn't call Maria Santissima because he didn't have the number.

When he got out, the police called me because Willie wanted to remove everything that contained the house and by the way he had sent the invitation to Michelle so that it was her and her husband who helped him. He then parked outside the fence surrounding the house, three trucks, a car and his van.

When I arrived at the house my son was not there and immediately, thinking he was alone, he called the Jean Pauls and the police, explaining that there were eight officers outside the house, including my husband, mentally ill who had just left the clinic, and wanted to take the things that belonged to the wedding and that he owned a gun, hidden in his van.

Four cars arrived, including one with metro captain Dade. So, Willie, he only took his clothes and staff and a reclining chair that his father had given him before he died. I realize how much an evil mind could achieve with cunning. Jean Paul arrived before the police and seeing that his sister was on the other side of the barricade, with her husband and Willie, he asked her:

"Why are you there instead of being with us as a family?"

That's a good question! - I added, but it was like throwing alcohol into the flames at that moment there. Theui and her sister said all the evil possible until Michelle left and my son and I entered the house, as the police sirens moved away ringing in the street.

I thought then, "This is what Willie wants, to deny friendship and love between brother and sister and daughter against mother... When Willie took his things, after living ten days in the van or at the home of friends, he came home because I let him. But only lived with us for two months as we had already started the divorce proceedings.

On the day of the divorce, he took the Jean Paul's with me to court, and when we entered, Willie as soon as he saw him spoke to the guard who was at the door, so as not to let him through. Jean Paul came in and said he was coming with me, so Willie, because he had gone wrong in his attempt, he was sarcastically speaking to him and they had a few words and the guard stopped to silence both of them.

When it was all over, Willie left so fast that he was no longer on view. He didn't know where he fucked. What a breath! I eror tolt at such a heavy weight from the stomach. Avevor a head full of thoughts, but they were oxen, I felt or free. If at that moment I had been told that stavor with Willie, he would have laughed and would not have believed it. But their onies of destiny are never known. All those years of mistreatment and suffering had not accustomed me not to be alone, as when er or younger and not Avevor fear of anything. Remember or that I had crossed an entire ocean that I was not even 17 years old, without speaking the language. I had arrived in Italy, which was a new world for me and I was not afraid or afraid in the face of new customs and customs, of a country as unknown and different as Europe. And then those films that I had starred in came back to me, I used to think about them while I was dancing or in love movies,

(ANY MOVIE SCENES)

Now, if I went out, I had to go home because it seemed to me that they were waiting for me, that I had to be there, if they wouldn't scold me. As time went on, little by little, I managed to free myself from that fear. He started going to a church where he met or a group of divorcees, from there from the SW that was called St. Agatha and with prayers, and the psychologist's speeches, we knew how to deal with life and how to spend day after day.

Now that I had the house, he had to keep it and what could be better than building a children's home on that big land, and if I had the house on the corner and already had a circular park, it would have been perfect to leave the children at the same door as the school. I had been informed that it had to have a fence throughout the courtyard, as required by law, 6 feet high so that there would be no problems with the escape of any of the children.

With these thoughts in mind, I called a loan company on the house, made an appointment and started paperwork for the loan, thus destroying my house for which he had fought so much and keeping my children living decently. In a short time, I received the phone call I expected from the mortgage company that wanted me to sign the documents for the new mortgage. I was euphoric, getting ready and leaving for the office. When I arrived, I was surprised that between his lawyer and the tax commission they took $12,000 and I only had $25,000 left. I thought:

"I can pay for anything and even with the children's house I can pay for it."

I had met a construction contractor in the church you were talking about and he called an architect who made the plans. After taking the measurements here and there, he said I had to move the septical pit. This pit was a short walk from the back entrance, I never liked the idea of having it so close to the house. Many times, Willie would say to me, "Why don't we move that sugar hole!"

When the man who cleaned it came with his truck and tank mounted behind the truck and began emptying it, the smell spread throughout the block. I closed the windows and didn't go out until it was all over.

What I didn't know was that one day not too far away, that pit would cost me the house. They wanted $3,000 to clean it, fill it up and put it somewhere else away from the house. The activity I Avevor planned to do was already costing me more than I had.

The architect had to obtain permits for everything: electricity, plumbing, including the happy well. Tired of waiting and the permits weren't coming, I decided to call someone who had recommended me. The boy came home, looked authentic, showing receipts, business cards and phones.

He set a deadline when these supposed to be over and I had to give him $1,000 to get started, another $1,000 at half-time and the last $1,000 at work finished. I signed a check for the agreed amount and the man left saying he had to finish a job he had already started and that next week he would come for sure.

On the other hand, the contractor who had commissioned the architect to make the plans wanted an advance to get permits from the state, in order to start construction and I gave it to him. Meanwhile, he starts buying various things for kindergarten. Since Willie had taken the VCR, I'd either bought another one and a 52-inch TV because I thought it was nice for kids to see Walt Disney movies.

I then told Michelle and Jean Paul a stereo for his used Chevette car that I had received from a friend of mine leaving for Venezuela and to complete my son's drive from a lawyer to fix the driver's license he hadn't paid for since 1985 and his license had been suspended.

The lawyer cost me $3,000 for everything but, after appearing twice in court, Jean Paul finally reissued his driver's license; he was a free man and no longer had to hide when he saw the police. I also took the badge, debt from the car and promised that one day I would get paid for that.

Jean Paul had realized that his father Robert was in the hospital doing some work in the hospital.

because he could not eat, with the result that he was cancerous. Finally, he had surgery, the tumor, and it was the size of an orange. Ricordo that Robert's sister had asked me to call her if he was to do and

the operation and I did it. And the sister and daughter of this one came. It was then that Michelle first met her cousin, who bore her name. For the occasione we went to the restaurant, Rain Forest Caffe. Dopo lunch they took pictures and went to the shops of el mall. After a short time, they couldn't stay any longer, and they left for France, Simome and Michelle. Even in those moments Sharon gave her the phone numbers to her average sister, Michelle and she also asked him, so year lost all contact. One day- 4 months before Robert's miserable life for nearly 2 years was over forever Michelle received a phone call that surprised her.

It was Sharon who was looking for her, thus finding in the telephone directory, two people with the same surname, began by asking,

"You have a sister named Sharon?..."

And Michelle replied, "Yes... Sharon, it's me!"

So, the two sisters found each other again. Sharon told me how badly Robert had seen it having also known that he had operated on the two hands of Carpal Tunnel making sure that he could not and work the plan with what was the way he earned his life. In June 2003, Michelle's eldest son, Max, was born and my daughter was home without work.

I went to social security to get Willi's pension and when I asked for Robert, just because his kids were looking for him, they told me the bill was in attivor because they couldn't give me the address. Robert tried to resume his career as a musicista invain, and with the antecedent he had in Fort Lauderdale, as ped or wire with his daughter Michelle, they said no, in the Miami Symphony Orchestra. After that he changed his house, leaving no one to indicate his name, so he lost count with his or her children. During this time Robert was diagnosed with colon cancer. Michell and knowing full well that she did not have much time to live went, together with Sharon, to see him and give him forgiveness for what he had done to her. With great force Michelle had managed to forgive.

"Michelle, did you come? I wasn't hoping. I know I hurt you, I know I was an infamous father to you. I loved your naivety. Who knows in you, maybe I see your mother again, you look a lot like her. She doesn't know, but I loved her. Then the days change. I've been wrong with her many, many times. Forgive me Michelle. Forgive me all."

Michelle said nothing, came up to him, shook his hand, and stroked it; it was the sweet hand of forgiveness. It seemed that Robert waited for that forgiveness, because the next day he died, perhaps a little more serene for that handshake and for that filial caress that now really made him feel like a father, thus ending the sad life he had lived until the last few years.

Now, with a serene mind, I see the past in small paintings, as if they were images of a puzzle that recomposes or as an old film made of beautiful and sometimes ugly moments of a lifetime; but I see them again in gusts, without any order of time... and places that are now far away.

I see ... who takes me to Italy for the cinema and reveals his true intentions by attempting violence, and so I see the tantiattori, in their mean machinations, in order to have my body, so Marin, Welles, Mature. And those who then in a great illusion make me an actress seem to give me seas and mountains and then exploit my economic success. How many illusions gives us the life that seems to give us joys and loves like Rod... which then vanishes, he as well, dileguandosi. How could I have imagined... Marry Robert such a refined man and then in the disappointment of every day. Robert, I see him in his turbulent abuse of my daughter, of our daughter. And imagining alone still gives me anger and pain, even in that Christian forgiveness of Michelle.

I see that friend who introduces me to Willie, and thinking of my children, who needed a father, in less than two months I marry him; a man with a criminal record, such as child abduction, wife rape and physical abuse. He suffers from epileptic seizures and takes Phenobarbital and Delantin but can't control himself. Yes, of course I should have had a hint of that personality of his but mistakes are often understood after having made them. I've been married to him for fifteen years, suffering mental and physical abuse, until I find the courage to divorce, but it's too late to rebuild a new life. At Homestead, where we moved, Willie has to drive 120 miles a day to get to work. And that's how he finds death by colliding head-on with another vehicle. Journalists write:

"The car flipped over and caught fire on Krome Avenue, the highway of death."

This contributes to the descent and destruction of Jean Paul and makes him addicted to tranquilizers, alcohol and drugs. Jean Paul felt alone in his efforts to fight his demons. In 2003, after many ups and downs, my son ended his one-year sentence in prison for driving with alcohol. On December 12, 2005, after taking some tranquilizer pills, at dawn, unable to drive and without someone to stop him, he died in a fatal head-on collision, and tragically died just like Willie. Jean Paul was only 39 years old.

In March 2001 I was diagnosed with breast cancer and I'm still fighting it.

This event is part of a series of horrendous episodes of my life; events that would make someone else surrender but not Alicia, the girl who became Bella Cortez and, despite so much harassment, abuse and exploitation became, in her time, a movie star.

Now it is precisely that world - sometimes regretful- that caresses my memories of when I was no longer the little Cuban girl but the queen of many films, made, even those, of dreams. Today I am recovering from cancer and I want to tell the facts of my life, offering a reason to learn from tragedies and savor those beautiful moments of life, albeitrare, that help us to move forward. But perhaps the secret of life lies in accepting it just as fate gives it to us without expecting anything more and without thinking about tomorrow.

For now, my story ends here but continues, silent in a secret dream that, who knows, one day I will tell or have told by a great writer only in a novel or who knows in a film; another flower, left in the drawer of the heart, to caress life that, sometimes is so bitter and at least once gives an enchanted gem, a pearl of a true love that becomes the unique reason to live, even to dream of a dream to be grasped, before it vanishes.

E N D

www.ingramcontent.com/pod-product-compliance
Lightning Source LLC
Chambersburg PA
CBHW022050050726
47591CB00002B/472